PAPER ART

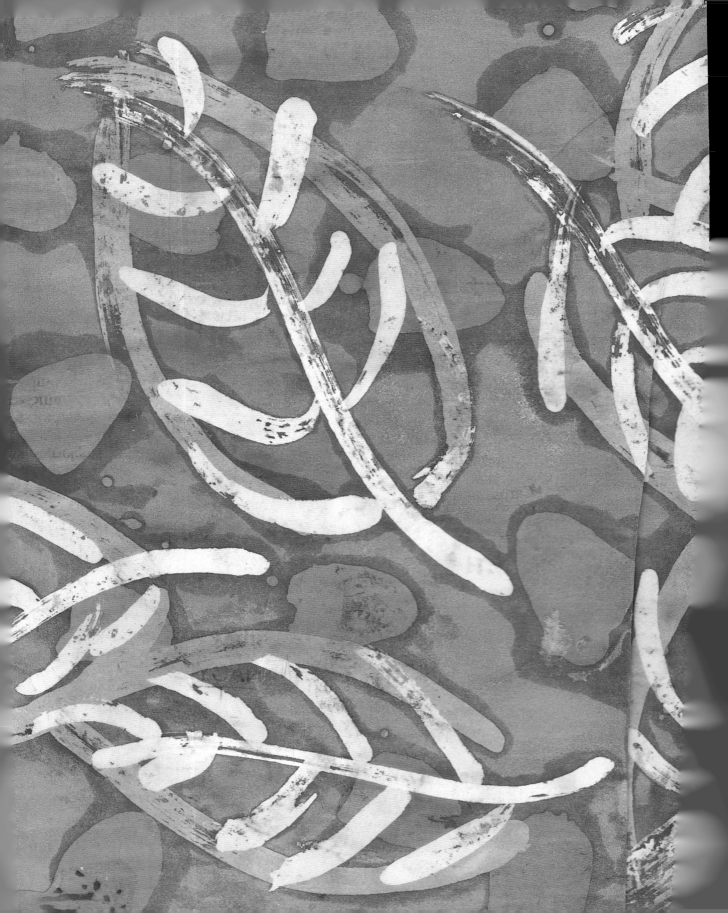

WATSON-GUPTILL ✄ CRAFTS

PAPER ART

The Complete Guide to Papercraft Techniques

Diane Maurer-Mathison

with Jennifer Philippoff

WATSON-GUPTILL PUBLICATIONS/NEW YORK

ACKNOWLEDGMENTS

Thanks to all the paper artists who shared their expertise and photographs of their inspiring work. Special thanks to Rona Chumbook and the following artists who invited us into their studios by providing us with photographs of their paper art in progress: Nancy Cook, Terri Fletcher, Shereen LaPlantz, Betsy Miraglia, Fred Mullett, and Mary Beth Ruby.

Notes on the Art

On page 1: "Celebration Paper Batik," a beaded and stitched paper batik by Billi R. S. Rothove. 33 × 14 1/2 inches (83.8 × 36.8 cm). Photo by Steve Ellis. See "Batik," page 80.

On pages 2–3: Batik paper by Jennifer Philippoff, 9 × 12 inches (22.7 × 30.5 cm). See "Batik," page 80.

On page 5: Sheet-cast paper rock sculpture by Jeanne Petrosky, 50 × 67 inches (127 × 170.2 cm). See "Cast Paper," page 28.

Senior Editor: Candace Raney
Edited by Joy Aquilino
Designed by Areta Buk
Graphic production by Ellen Greene

Copyright © 1997 by Diane Maurer-Mathison

First published in 1997 by Watson-Guptill Publications, a division of BPI Communications, Inc., 1515 Broadway, New York, N.Y. 10036

Library of Congress Cataloging-in-Publication Data
Maurer-Mathison, Diane V., 1944–
    Paper art: the complete guide to papercraft techniques / Diane Maurer-Mathison with Jennifer Philippoff.
       p.   cm. — (Watson-Guptill crafts)
    Includes bibliographical references and index.
    ISBN 0-8230-3840-8 (flexiback)
    1. Paperwork. I. Philippoff, Jennifer, 1964–   . II. Title.
III. Series.
TT870.M38   1997
745.54—dc21   97-28466
                                               CIP

Manufactured in Hong Kong

First printing, 1997

1 2 3 4 5 6 7 8 9 / 05 04 03 02 01 00 99 98 97

For Jeff

Contents

Preface

Work on *Paper Art* ironically began when I was invited to give a fabric marbling demonstration in a college class. The course was called "Surface Design on Fabric" and students had produced exciting works with sophisticated stamping, stitching, beading, printing, and pole-wrapped dyeing experiments. When I wondered aloud whether the techniques could be used on paper, I got little response except for a few knitted eyebrows. Finally one student spoke for the class. "Why put it on paper, when you can put it on fabric?" Although I enjoy good design on any surface, my focus is paper, and I left determined to find other artists who produce equally rich surface designs on paper.

An invitation to create a slide show for a marbling convention provided me with an excuse to continue the quest and unearth the revolutionary paper artists I imagined cloistered in their studios. I placed ads in book arts, papermaking, and papercraft journals, asking artists who were creating innovative surface design on paper to contact me. Word of mouth carried my request throughout the United States. Soon I had slides and photos of amazing handmade, stamped, sculpted, beaded, and even shibori-dyed

Some of the many domestic and imported handmade papers available today include papers from Germany, India, Italy, Japan, and Thailand.

paperworks. The slide show "Beyond Marbling: Surface Design on Paper" was a success, and brought me news of even more people quietly pursuing paper as a craft and fine-art medium.

My marbling workshops soon expanded into decorative paper workshops, where the enthusiasm of students for exploring new ways of making, decorating, and manipulating paper convinced me that many others shared my passion.

So here's the book so many people encouraged me to write. *Paper Art* is a technique book, full of photos of leading paper artists' work, with many step-by-step photos of paper artists at work. Some of the techniques, like paste design and leaf printing, are easy to master; others, like paper cutting and sculpture, require more effort to get professional results. You can grow with this book, creating more complex works as you master new techniques. *Paper Art* is designed to entice novices into trying a new craft, encourage working paper artists to experiment with new techniques, and convince fiber artists to try "putting it on paper."

From "A Meadow Series" by Wayne A. O. Fuerst. Detail of a 33- × 78-inch (83.8- × 198-cm) landscape created by squirting and pouring colored pulp onto a couched sheet of paper. Wayne's mastery of pulp painting allows him to use squeeze bottles like artist's brushes, rendering even the finest detail, like a delicate tree branch, in pulp.

1 PAPERMAKING

True paper probably didn't exist until about A.D. 105, when Ts'ai Lun, a member of the Chinese Han Dynasty, invented it. The art of papermaking was introduced to Japan via Korea early in the 7th century. In Japan, handmade paper or *washi* was considered a sacred material, but because of its strength it had practical uses too.

Papermaking was introduced into the Arab world in 751 when the Arabs, attacked by the Chinese in Samarkand, found that some of their captives were harboring an important secret: how to make paper. As knowledge of the new-found craft spread quickly throughout the Islamic world, papermaking centers were established in Baghdad, Cairo, and Damascus.

The European community endured the expense of importing paper from the Arabs for several hundred years until the 12th century, when papermaking became known in Spain. A hundred years later, the famous Italian Fabriano mill was built. By the 15th century, paper mills were operating in France, Germany, and England. In 1690, the first American paper mill was built in Germantown, Pennsylvania.

Today, sheets of handmade paper are once again revered for their texture, form, and weight, from tissue-thin with delicate deckle edges, to thick and bulky, resembling the bark from which they may still be made. All manner of ingredients may be used to create papers, or to enhance the texture of a sheet. The use of inserts placed on molds allow papermakers the freedom to create papers in virtually any shape they choose. One of the strongest and most versatile materials available to artists and craftspeople, paper pulp can be woven, sculpted, colored, and carved. Diluted pulp can be squirted onto a mold to produce a painting, or cast into a shape to amuse or inspire.

Modern papermaking is more than a resurgence of an ancient craft, it has become a revolutionary new art medium.

Handmade papers can have a sophisticated elegance or be wildly eccentric, depending upon the whims of the papermaker.

Making Your Own Paper

The first step in making paper is to beat the torn-up recycled papers, plant fibers, or linters (pulp in sheet form) to a pulp. The pulp is then mixed with water in the papermaking vat or tub to form a *slurry.* The papermaker next dips the basic papermaking equipment—the *mold and deckle*—into the vat and lifts it out horizontally to capture some of the floating pulp on the screened surface of the mold. Holding the deckle (a kind of fence that corrals the pulp) in place, the papermaker shakes the mold from front to back and side to side to help weave the settling fibers into a mat. When the water has drained through the screen, the deckle is removed and the matted fibers are *couched,* or transferred to a dampened cloth or felt. When the fibers are pressed and dried, they will have completed their metamorphosis into a sheet of paper.

To begin making your own paper, you can purchase professional equipment from a papermaking supplier or improvise by using common household items.

BASIC EQUIPMENT

- *Kitchen blender.* You'll need a basic blender for macerating the fiber to make the paper pulp. Look for one at a garage sale that you can reserve for papermaking only.
- *Large dishpan or plastic storage container.* Either of these can serve as a papermaking vat. It should be about 8 inches (20.3 cm) deep and large enough to accommodate the mold and deckle and give you room to maneuver.
- *Mold and deckle.* The mold and matching deckle determine the size and shape of the sheet of paper made. Improvised molds can be made by stretching nylon net curtain material over a round embroidery frame or by using nonrusting staples to attach the net to a picture frame. Matching frames without netting can be used as deckles to contain the pulp. Eventually, however, you'll want to treat yourself to a professional mold and deckle that is durable enough to last through years of papermaking. Purchase one through one of the papermaking houses listed in the source directory at the back of this book, or construct one that will stand up to repeated immersions by reinforcing the corners well and waterproofing the wood used.
- *Sponges.* Sponges are used for cleanup and to help release ornery sheets from the mold.
- *Couching cloths.* Dressmaker's sew-in interfacing or old cotton sheets can be used to support newly formed sheets of paper. These should be slightly larger than the paper you intend to make. Handiwipes can also be used if you don't mind the slight pattern they impart to the papers.

Susan Gosin feeding the Hollander beater at Dieu Donné Papermill.

Letting a sheet of paper drain while making another at Dieu Donné Papermill.

Susan Gosin lifting the mold after couching a sheet of paper at Dieu Donné Papermill.

- *Couching felts.* Thicker and more absorbent than couching cloths, couching felts support and help draw water from the wet stack of papers. Either old army blankets or purchased felts will do. The felts should be about 2 inches (5.1 cm) larger on all sides than the papers you make.
- *Press boards.* You'll need two of these, which should be made from Formica or urethaned wood. They should be slightly larger than your paper mold. These will sandwich your *post* (a stack of couched sheets) and, with the help of two C-clamps (or one heavy body standing on them), remove most of the water from your newly formed sheets of paper. A simple paper press made from bolts and wood (see page 20) is the most efficient way to press a stack of wet paper.
- *Large shallow tub.* This piece of equipment can be used to catch the water pressed out of the paper. (You can omit this if you work outdoors.)

Some of the equipment and materials used to make handmade paper.

- *Sheet of Plexiglas or Formica.* Either of these makes a good drying surface for the paper and imparts a smooth surface to one side of the sheet.
- *Large flat brush.* This helps transfer the pressed sheet to the drying surface.
- *Plastic sheeting and plastic apron.* These will come in handy—papermaking is a very wet process.
- *Strainer and mesh curtain material.* You can use these to strain out the extra pulp at the end of your papermaking session and store it for later use.
- *Gloves (optional).* Latex exam gloves are recommended not only for those people whose skin becomes irritated when exposed to water for prolonged periods, but to prevent staining from pigments when creating colored sheets with dyes (see page 24). The latex is thin enough that it won't interfere with your sense of touch. Heavier rubber gloves should be used when handling caustic chemicals such as soda ash, which is used for pulping raw plant materials (see page 22); a mask and goggles are also recommended for this procedure.

BASIC MATERIALS

The *furnish,* which is the raw material from which paper is made, can come from several sources:
- *Sheets of pulp.* Abaca (from banana leaf fibers) or cotton linters (pulp in sheet form) can be ordered from papermaking supply houses. These are easy to use and produce fine papers.
- *Recycled paper.* Computer paper, photocopy paper, old blotters, pieces of drawing paper, mountboard, and typing paper can all be used to make handmade paper. Newspapers and magazines should be avoided, as they are highly acidic and will produce inferior sheets that are weak and will eventually turn brittle. Unprinted paper is best, unless you want to incorporate stray letters as a design element.
- *Plant fibers.* Although many garden plants and weeds contain long cellulose fibers ideal for making paper, preparing the plant material can be very time-consuming and often involves laborious chopping, handbeating, and soaking, or using chemicals like caustic soda. Instructions for using plant fibers as decorative accents in paper and recommendations for using plant fibers that can be easily broken down appear later in this chapter (see pages 24 and 22, respectively).
- *Water.* Sometimes mineral or organic compounds in water will cause brown stains to appear in a dried sheet. Use purified or distilled water for papermaking if you have high levels of minerals like iron, copper, or manganese in your tap water.

MAKING A MOLD AND DECKLE

The inside dimensions of your mold will determine the size of the paper made. The following directions can be used to create a mold and deckle that will produce sheets measuring 8½ × 11 inches (21.6 × 27.9 cm).

1. Purchase two 8-foot-long (2.44-m-long) strips of wood that are ¾ inches (1.91 cm) square and cut two 12½-inch (31.8-cm) strips and two 8½-inch (21.6-cm) strips to create the mold frame. Miter the corners and glue them with a waterproof glue. When the glue is dry, sand the wood smooth and nail the corners with brass nails. Reinforce the corner joints with brass L-shaped braces. Apply two coats of waterproofing urethane. Let dry thoroughly.

2. Cut brass or aluminum screen slightly smaller than the outside dimensions of your mold, then use nonrusting staples to stretch it over the frame. (The L-shaped braces should be on the *opposite* side of the frame.) Work from the middle of each side toward the edges to stretch the screen taut. Cover the staples and edges of the screen with waterproof tape to prevent pulp from migrating under the wire during use. NOTE: Fiberglass window screen can also be used if it is stretched over the top and down the outside edge of the frame to get it taut before stapling.

3. To create the deckle, build another frame exactly like the mold, but don't cover it with screen. Be sure to waterproof the deckle, too.

Plans for constructing a sturdy mold and deckle. Squared-off or mitered corners are fine, as long as they are joined securely.

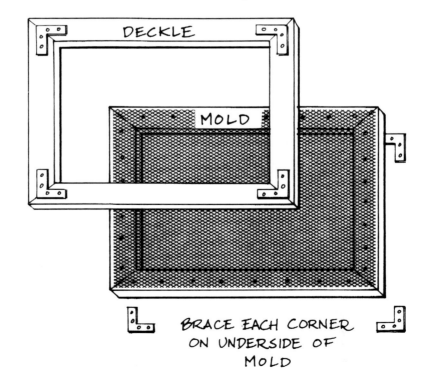

DECKLE

MOLD

BRACE EACH CORNER ON UNDERSIDE OF MOLD

PREPARING THE PULP

Using Linters. Wet several linters and tear them into 1-inch (2.5-cm) pieces. Add a small handful of torn linters to a blender two-thirds full of warm water. (As a general rule of thumb, use about 1 part linters to 2 parts warm water.) Beat for about 1 minute, using short bursts of speed to avoid straining the blender motor.

When your pulp is the proper consistency, it will be free of clumps and knots and the individual fibers will appear to be suspended, cloudlike, in the water. Place about 1 tablespoon (15 ml) of blender pulp in a glass of water to see if it's well macerated, then empty the blended pulp into your papermaking vat and add about two more blendersful of water. Continue beating and pouring into your vat, adding more water each time, until you have about 1 pint (473 ml) of concentrated pulp mixed with 4 gallons (15.1 l) of water. You needn't be too concerned with exact proportions. The ratio of pulp to water can be adjusted to create thinner or thicker sheets of paper by adding more water or concentrated pulp to your vat.

Using Recycled Papers. Tear light- to medium-weight papers into 1-inch (2.5-cm) pieces and soak them overnight in water. Heavy watercolor paper needs to be torn into smaller pieces and soaked for several days. For very heavy paper or mountboard, an even longer soaking time or boiling may be necessary. Lightweight papers will probably only need to be beaten for about 15 seconds, while heavier materials will have to be macerated longer to adequately separate the fibers.

Adding wet torn linters to the blender for pulping.

FORMING A SHEET

Stir the slurry in your vat with your hand to distribute the pulp evenly. Place the edge of your deckle on top of the screened side of your mold so that the flat edges are together. Hold the deckle in place with your thumbs and grasp the bottom of the mold with your fingers. If your mold is rectangular, place your hands in position on the short sides.

Hold the mold and deckle at a slight angle and lower them into the vat at its far edge. Then bring the mold and deckle toward you, shifting them to a horizontal position and holding them level for a moment just below the water's surface before lifting them swiftly up and out of the vat.

As the water drains through the screen, gently shake the mold and deckle from side to side and from front to back to disperse and mesh the pulp fibers you've scooped up. When most of the water has drained back into the vat, tilt the mold and deckle slightly to let additional excess water drain off. Rest your mold and deckle on the edge of the vat and carefully remove the deckle, making sure you don't drip water on your newly formed sheet of paper.

If you do accidentally drip water on the sheet, which may cause a thin spot or hole, or if your first sheet appears thick in one area and thin in another, place the mold pulp side down on the surface of the slurry to "kiss off" the sheet back into the vat. This action will cause the sheet to break down into floating pulp again.

The smooth, continuous motion that produces a uniform sheet of paper will come with a little practice. Judging how much pulp to add to the water in your vat will also come with experience. In general, if your paper seems too thick, add more water to the vat. If it's too thin (as it will be after you've made several sheets), add more beaten pulp to it.

To scoop up pulp for a sheet of handmade paper, lower the mold and deckle into the far end of the vat at a slight angle. Then shift the mold and deckle to a horizontal position before lifting them up and out of the vat.

COUCHING

After you've removed the deckle from the mold, it's time to couch (rhymes with "pooch") the sheet. Couching (from the French word *coucher,* which means "to lay down") refers to the act of transferring the newly formed sheet of paper from the mold to the dampened couching cloth or felt.

To prepare a couching pad, place a dampened felt on your press board and place another dampened piece of couching cloth on top of the felt. The thickness of the pad provides enough suction to start the process of drawing water from the papers. Smooth out any wrinkles in the cloth, stand your mold upright at its right edge, then roll the mold down firmly onto it. When the left edge of the mold makes contact with the cloth, lift the right edge up. Usually the slight rocking motion releases the sheet of paper. (If you have difficulty getting the paper to release at first, place the mold face down on the couching cloth and use a wet sponge to press and loosen the back of the sheet through the mold screen.)

When the sheet is successfully couched, dampen another couching cloth and place it on top of the wet sheet of paper. Your next piece of handmade paper will be couched on top of this cloth. To build up a post of papers, continue couching and adding dampened cloths until you've created a stack of about ten sheets. Then add another thick felt to the top of the stack and cover it with the other press board.

Stand the mold upright at the edge of the couching cloth and roll it firmly down to release the handmade sheet.

PRESSING

The simplest way to press out the water from your post of papers is to stand on the top press board for about 10 minutes. If you'd rather be freed up for greater adventures, you can make a simple paper press like the one shown below. By using strips of wood and bolts with wing nuts, you can encase and apply pressure to the paper post. C-clamps can also be placed on the stack and tightened to press out moisture. Regardless of which pressing method you choose, be sure to elevate the post of papers in a larger tub or kitty litter pan to allow the water to drain away.

This paper press consists of two strips of waterproofed wood and bolts with wing nuts used to apply pressure to the post of papers.

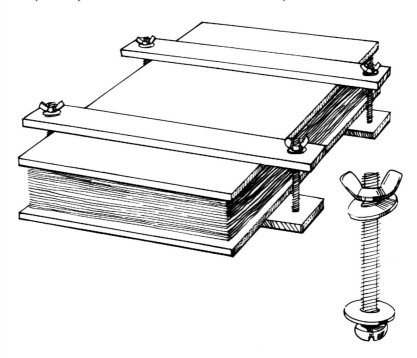

DRYING

When most of the moisture has been pressed out of your handmade papers, you can transfer them to a flat drying surface such as glass, Plexiglas, or Formica. Transport each sheet on its couching cloth and use a wide, flat brush to gently brush the back of the cloth to coax the sheet onto the drying surface. Then peel off the couching cloth. Allow the sheet to remain in position until it is completely dry. You can also pin each couching cloth with a damp sheet still attached to Styrofoam or urethaned wood and let the sheets air-dry. If you're in a rush, a third alternative is to place each pressed sheet between blotters and iron them dry.

Once the sheets of handmade paper are dry, they can be stacked and put under some books or boards for several days to flatten them.

Gently brush the back of the couching cloth to transfer the pressed paper to the Plexiglas. Then peel off the couching cloth and let the paper air-dry.

SIZING YOUR PAPER

Paper without any sizing, which is called *waterleaf,* is very absorbent. Although waterleaf may be enjoyed as a piece of artwork, used in a paper craft, or used for further decorative techniques like stamping with gouache-based paints, printing, or marbling, many inks will feather or bleed when applied to it. To use a handmade sheet with calligraphy inks, for example, you'll need to *size* it, or coat it to make it stronger and less absorbent.

Sizing may be added to a sheet either *internally,* by adding it to the vat, or *externally,* by brushing or spraying it on dry paper. Gelatin, household starch, Liquid Hercon 70 sizing, or methyl cellulose can all be used for internal sizing. If you already have some methyl cellulose on hand from marbling or making paste papers, dissolve 1 tablespoon (15 ml) in a little water until it becomes a thick jelly. Then dilute it with 2 quarts (1.9 l) of water. You can add this to the vat or spray it on thoroughly dry paper. Another option is to spray dry papers with an artists' fixative. It's easiest and safest, however, to follow directions provided with sizing materials from a papermaking supply house.

CLEANUP

Use a strainer or mesh fabric to strain out any pulp that's left in your vat after papermaking before pouring the liquid down the drain. If you have some pulp left over, you can compress it into balls and let it dry out or freeze it for later use. Molds, deckles, and other equipment should be hosed down and any wayward pulp picked off. Pay attention to felts and couching cloths, brushing off any remaining bits of pulp and washing cloths as needed.

If you've used sizing or methyl cellulose in your vat to strengthen casting pulp (see "Cast Paper," page 28), be sure to wash your felts and cloths.

Pulping Fresh Plant Materials

Many plants can be used to make paper, but some take hours of preparation and caustic chemicals to break them down and dissolve out the undesirable parts of the plant. Others, like rhubarb, celery, and cauliflower leaves, can be cut into 1- to 2-inch (2.5- to 5.1-cm) pieces, soaked in water for several hours, then simmered in a stainless steel or enamel pot for another hour or so to prepare them for pulping.

The leaves and stems of tougher plants often need to be cut into small pieces, soaked overnight in warm water to soften them, and then simmered with soda ash for several hours until their fibers separate easily. A common ratio is to add 1 tablespoon (15 ml) of soda ash to the water in which the pieces have been soaked for every ¼ pound (113 g) of dry fiber used. (You'll need to wear rubber gloves, a NIOSH-approved mask for dusts and mists, and goggles when working with soda ash, as it can cause burns.) When the plant fibers can be pulled apart easily—after at least 4 hours (perhaps longer for woody plants)—they are ready to be washed in cold water until all traces

Cooking Alabama kozo bark on a gas burner at the University of Alabama in Tuscaloosa. The bark is cooked with an amount of soda ash equal to about 20 percent of the weight of the bark for 2 hours to prepare it for beating. Photo by Lynn Amlie.

of soda ash are eliminated and the water runs clear. You may now want to handbeat your cooked plant fibers against a board with a wooden mallet or beating stick to decrease the amount of time you must spend macerating them in a blender, which weakens them.

To create your own plant-fiber paper recipes, experiment by soaking and cooking vegetables or nontoxic garden plants and adding them to your linter pulp or using them as a base for the pulp. If you live in the city or suburbs, visit farmer's markets and florist shops for castoffs to use in your papermaking. If you live in the country, you can grow or scavenge materials. Denise DeMarie, an Oregon papermaker, makes her sheets almost exclusively from problem weeds and agricultural by-products.

The Japanese are masters at forming papers from a variety of plants, including gampi, kozo, and mitsumata. Some excellent books that describe papermaking using Oriental techniques are listed in the suggested readings at the back of this book.

Beating the cooked kozo bark with a stick until the individual fibers separate. Photo by Lynn Amlie.

Some of Denise DeMarie's papers made from problem weeds and agricultural by-products (clockwise from left): estuary grass, corn plant, spring spartina with flowers, salvaged cedar bark with kozo, and summer spartina (center).

Adding Color and Texture

Handmade papers that derive their color and texture from the plants used to create them have a natural elegance, but it's fun to create more lively, colorful sheets by accenting them with natural and manmade embellishments.

USING PLANT MATERIALS

Plant material such as flowers, leaves, and ferns can be added to your pulp to give it color and texture. Purchased dried flowers sometimes contain chemicals that can cause paper discoloration, but many fresh flowers can be preserved for future papermaking sessions by drying them in a microwave for about 3 minutes or by letting them air-dry in bunches. To use them, just sprinkle the dried material into the vat of abaca or cotton linter pulp and scoop them up on the mold as you form each sheet.

Fresh flowers and foliage will sometimes bleed or stain a sheet of paper as it dries. To counteract this process, simmer the fresh plant material in water for about 10 minutes before you add it to the vat, which will extract any color that could migrate to your paper.

Pressed flowers, bits of dried onion skins, coconut, or corn silk, seeds, spices, and even tea leaves can be added to the slurry to enhance the sheet. The plant materials can also be placed on top of a freshly couched sheet and a thin mixture of pulp and water can be squirted on top of them with a squeeze bottle or turkey baster to help them adhere to the sheet.

ADDING FABRICS, FOILS, AND OTHER DECORATIVE FRAGMENTS

Strips of iridescent fabric or ribbon can be cut and glitzy colored threads unraveled and added to the slurry to give a sheet added pizzazz. Confetti, glitter, sequins, pieces of other decorative papers, lace, and colorful foils— just about anything that's relatively flat and lightweight—can be added to the vat or embedded in a sheet to help give it color and texture. For the ultimate in recycling, tear pieces of an abandoned paper wasp's nest and add them to your paper.

ADDING COLOR TO YOUR SHEETS

One way to add color to your handmade paper is to add colored paper to your pulp. Recycled photocopy paper can yield interesting colors. You can also try coloring your pulp with fabric dyes such as Rit, Procion, and Dylon, or with vegetable and acrylic dyes. Because paper pulp is made of natural fibers, most dyes that will color cotton or linen can be used. For the most intense and predictable results, however, your best bet is to invest in some of the dyes available through a papermaking supplier.

When petals and leaves are added to paper pulp, or held in place with a thin layer of pulp, lovely flower-inclusion papers can be made. These rich handmade sheets, with flowers imbedded in abaca and cotton linters, are by Wayne A. O. Fuerst and Jay W. Luiz.

The bright colors of Claudia Lee's handmade postcards are achieved with pigment dyes.

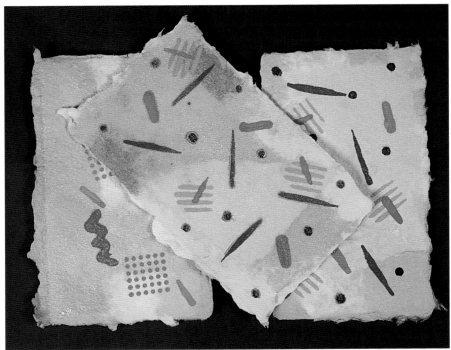

Making Shaped Papers

We often think of paper as having a rectangular shape, with deckle edges if it's handmade. By making your own paper, you gain the freedom to create sheets in any size or shape. The possibilities for unique cards, books, and paper art are endless.

CREATING A SHAPED DECKLE

One way to create unusual shaped papers is to cut a design—a triangle, for instance—out of a sheet of foamcore board to create a shaped deckle. Waterproof the foamcore board by coating it with urethane, let it dry, then hold it against the mold as you dip it into the vat. The pulp will settle on the screen only in the opening you've created. Your efforts will be rewarded with a triangular piece of paper.

To make a template for an envelope, first trim the edges of your foamcore board to match the outside dimensions of your mold frame. Open an envelope and lay it in the center of your foamcore board. Trace around the envelope, then cut out the shape with an X-Acto knife. Urethane the new deckle to waterproof it.

Although it's a bit more expensive than foamcore board, Buttercut, a product available from Lee S. McDonald, Inc., is great for making shaped deckles. It's waterproof and flexible and has an adhesive backing that can be placed directly on the mold to block out areas of the screen.

Shaped papers can be made by blocking out parts of the mold with specially designed deckles made from Buttercut or foamcore board.

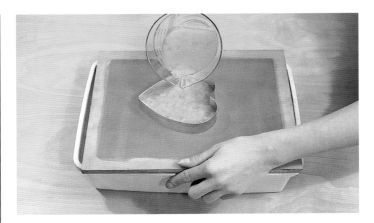

Using a cookie cutter as a deckle to create a heart-shaped paper.

You can also use a cookie cutter as a deckle to create a shaped paper. Just place your mold over a bucket or sink, put the cookie cutter on the mold and pour diluted pulp into the center of the cookie cutter. Let the pulp drain thoroughly, then lift off the makeshift deckle. Couch, press, and dry the cookie-shaped paper, or couch it onto a contrasting couched sheet to laminate them.

MAKING FREE-FORM PAPERS

Papers don't have to conform to the shape of a mold and deckle at all. If you couch one wet sheet over another at an odd angle the sheets will laminate and bond together during pressing and drying. Extra-long sheets made from different colored pulp can be created this way, too.

Claudia Lee's delightful haphazardly shaped papers are made by couching one sheet over another at odd angles.

Cast Paper

Paper casting is a great way to create lightweight yet very dramatic relief sculptures. By casting pulp into a mold or over an armature, you can create paper with a specific shape and depth.

USING FOUND MOLDS

Found molds like seashells or animal- and foliage-shaped muffin pans and candy molds can be used to make handcast hanging ornaments, decorations for greeting cards, or components for larger works.

To create a thick casting material, lift some pulp from your vat and strain it to remove some of the water. Apply the pulp with your hands and press it evenly into your mold, letting some of it extend, if you like, to create a deckle edge. Use a damp sponge to apply pressure to compact the pulp and wick off some of the moisture. Wring the sponge out as you work. Removing more moisture will lessen drying time, which can take several days.

When the cast paper is dry, peel it from the mold. If necessary, use a dull knife to help ease it out. If you have difficulty getting your mold to release, next time try coating it with a nonstick cooking spray such as Pam and then rinsing it with warm water before applying the pulp. Butcher's wax or a commercial release agent available from a papermaking supplier can also be used. Try casting with pulps that have been dyed different colors to create variegated works.

SHEET CASTING

If couched sheets of paper are sponged to remove most of the water, they can be draped over sticks, rods, and plasticine sculptures or eased into forms such as masks, plaster molds, or even antique brooches. To build up a stronger laminated structure, tear off strips of the couched sheet and place them in position on your casting form. Overlap the feathered edges of the torn sheets as you press them in place with a sponge or tamp them into place with a small stiff-bristled brush. The feathered edges help create a strong bond and diminish the visibility of seams in your finished work.

Some papermakers like to add methyl cellulose to their pulp to give the casting more bonding strength and create a stiffer paper. Since methyl cellulose is also a glue, however, adding it can sometimes make removing cast paper from detailed molds more difficult.

You can work with colored pulp, or paint the cast paper after it is dry. Barbara Fletcher's amazing whimsical cast paper sculptures are made by pressing sheets of recycled handmade paper into plaster molds in several layers. When the cast paper is dry, she removes it from the mold and colors the sculpture with Procion dyes to give it intense color and luminosity. Barbara then coats the work with acrylic medium to make it more durable.

Press the strained pulp into a found mold with your hands. Use a sponge to apply pressure and remove some of the moisture. (Our mold was coated with urethane to help it release the paper.)

The intense color of Barbara Fletcher's whimsical "Fish Lips" masks is the result of painting the dry cast paper with Procion dyes. The large mask is 8¹/₂ × 6¹/₂ × 5 inches (21.6 × 16.5 × 12.7 cm).

Pulp Painting

If you water down colored pulp so that it's extra runny and place it in a turkey baster or plastic squeeze bottle, you can paint or draw with it. Geometric, representational, or artful abstract paintings can be made. Available from papermaking suppliers, Formation Aid, a substance that helps suspend and evenly disperse the pulp's fibers, giving them more time to interlock, helps keep the pulp from clogging the applicator nozzle. Work directly by squirting pulp on a couched sheet of paper or draw on the mold and then couch onto a newly formed sheet.

Using a grid or stencil such as a cake cooling rack can help define areas to fill with different colored pulps to get you started making patterned papers. To create her intricate pigment-colored pulp paintings, Betsy Miraglia draws a design on Plexiglas with watercolor crayons, inverts the Plexiglas, and lays on small handfuls of pulp, side by side, to fill in the sketched design. Betsy provided the photos demonstrating the process involved in producing "A Prayer for Grace," shown opposite, below.

Betsy creates a crayon drawing of the design for "A Prayer for Grace" on thin Plexiglas, then flips the Plexiglas over. Since the finished side of the artwork will be face down on the Plexiglas, Betsy will be creating the design in reverse, too.

Betsy places slightly strained pulp over the drawing to a ¹/₄-inch (6-mm) thickness. She uses found tools such as dental tools, wooden skewers, and plastic wallpaper corners to push the pulp into position. The manipulated pulp is then lightly sponged to remove water.

When the work is completed, the entire piece is sprayed with water and the back of the work is strengthened with individual sheets of slightly sponged handmade paper (shown over a section of the work here). Next, nonwoven interfacing, which has a texture-free, neutral surface, is laid over the work and gently sponged to press it to an even thickness. Then a synthetic chamois cloth is applied overnight to remove excess water. Demo photos by Judy Smith-Kressley.

"A Prayer for Grace" by Betsy Miraglia, 32 × 40 inches (81.3 × 101.6 cm). Once the work has completely air-dried, it releases easily from the Plexiglas and can finally be viewed from the right side.

2 DECORATING PAPER

The art of decorating paper has been practiced for centuries. The Chinese, the first culture to develop papermaking, introduced most of the decorative paper techniques still in use today. By the 7th century, the Chinese were already stamping paper with wood, horn, and bamboo; cutting and stenciling paper; and possibly marbling it, too. As artisans in other countries learned of these and other means of embellishing paper, they developed their own colors and styles of decorating based on images reflected by their culture and geography.

If you visit a museum with a decorative paper collection or the rare book room of a university library, you can see many of the historic marbled, block-printed, and paste-designed papers produced hundreds of years ago. If you take pencil and paper with you, you can jot down notes on patterns and motifs that interest you and use them as inspiration in planning your own decorative papers. Books on ornament and design can also offer a starting point for stenciled, stamped, or printed designs, as can a trip to a fabric or wallpaper store. Wrapping papers, too, can generate ideas for your patterned papers. Another option is to begin playing with the tools and materials for a new technique and remain open to the images that evolve naturally.

If you're designing a paper with a particular end use in mind, that alone can give you design ideas. If a stencil paper will be used for a lamp shade on a lamp with an art deco base, you would probably want to come up with a stencil design that repeated an art deco motif. If a decorative paper is to be used on a frame for a wedding photo, an embossed Celtic knot would be more appropriate than a repeat pattern of rubber stamped tigers. (Unless, of course, the bride happens to be a zoo director.) Eventually you may find a definite graphic style and adopt color combinations that easily identify you as the artist.

"Fish Tales" by Betsy Miraglia, 50 × 60 inches (127 × 152.4 cm). Acrylic stenciling, clay, and waxed linen accent this pulp painting.

Surface Design and Color

Printmaking, a popular art and graphic medium, can yield satisfying results without the use of a traditional printing press. Printing blocks, too, can be made of nontraditional materials instead of being made exclusively from wood and battleship linoleum. Many other materials, like vegetables, sponges, and leaves, can be used to create images to enjoy as prints or to use as all-over repeat designs for decorative paper. Other paper art techniques, such as paste paper design, batik, orizomegami, and marbling, will broaden your surface design repertoire. Explore techniques individually, but also try combining some—paste design and stamping, for instance—for really unique papers.

DESIGN PRINCIPLES

By making repeat patterns with a square raised ink pad or other printing device you can discover design principles used in printmaking and other forms of paper decoration. Notice how movement and rhythm, so important to a work, vary, as you place the prints closer together or farther apart. The color of the printed square will also help determine whether it recedes into the background of a design or becomes a focal point. Warm colors usually appear to move forward, while cool ones tend to recede.

Changing color intensity also influences rhythm and helps prevent repeat patterns from becoming boring. The amount of ink and pressure you apply when making a print determines how light or dark the print will be and how much of the paper color will show through the printed area. The contrast between the images helps carry a viewer's eye through a design.

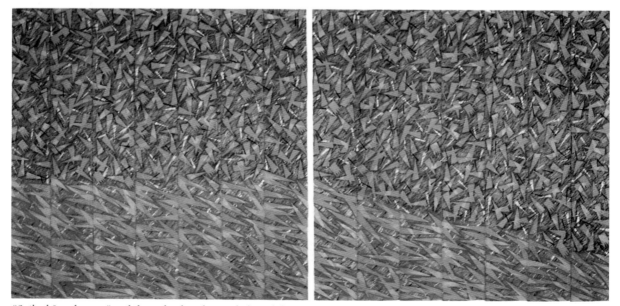

"Spiked Landscape," a shibori-dyed and stenciled work by Terri Fletcher measuring 41 × 82 inches (104 × 208.3 cm).

Remember that the *negative* or unprinted areas between squares or other images also define a shape and will hold the viewer's eye as much as the printed ones. Try overlapping images in various ways or alternating the direction of the print from row to row. Don't worry about having images line up exactly. Try to relax and explore whatever medium you're working in. Later, when you feel more comfortable, you can lightly rule pencil lines to make temporary registration marks if you want to be more precise.

COLOR MIXING

If you don't have experience mixing colors, an inexpensive color mixing guide will come in handy. By referring to the color wheel shown below, you can see how mixing just the *primary colors*—red, blue, and yellow—can yield a range of other hues. The term "primary" refers to the fact that red, blue, and yellow, which serve as the basis for all other colors, cannot be created by mixing any other colors. In addition to the three primaries, the color wheel shows the three *secondary colors*—purple, orange, and green—which are obtained by mixing two primaries (for example, red + blue = purple), and the six *tertiary colors*, which are obtained by mixing a primary with an adjacent secondary (for example, red + orange = red-orange). Your palette can be further extended by changing these colors' value (making them darker or lighter), either by *tinting* (adding white) or *shading* (adding black).

A color mixing guide can show you the results of mixing colors in various proportions—a great help if you're trying to reproduce color combinations from a favorite swatch of jungle print fabric or a pastel colorplate in a historic design book.

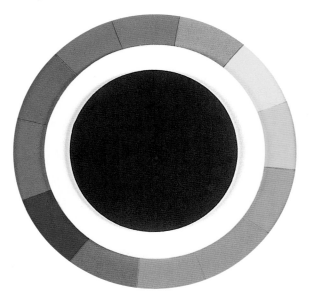

An infinite number of hues can be created by mixing the primary colors red, blue, and yellow. This color wheel also includes secondary and tertiary colors.

Embossing

Embossing creates a raised or recessed surface in a sheet of paper to give it a decorative pattern or textured surface. Three types of embossing can be used to decorate paper: wet embossing, dry embossing, and thermal embossing (which is discussed separately under "Stamping" on page 49).

WET EMBOSSING

The first type, wet embossing, includes working with newly formed sheets of paper that have been pressed to remove some of the moisture, and working with other papers (not necessarily handmade) that have been dampened to make them receptive to materials pressed into them.

To wet-emboss a sheet of paper, you'll need the following materials and equipment:

- *Paper.* A handmade paper or a good-quality paper like Canson, Strathmore, or Rives works best for this technique.
- *Two waterproofed press boards.* You can use the same ones used for papermaking (see page 14), unless you prefer to work larger.
- *Embossing materials.* Beans, rice, string, lace, pieces of berry baskets, plastic floor runners, unmounted rubber stamps—almost anything that is relatively flat with raised or cut-out areas to impart texture or pattern can be used for embossing.
- *Couching felt or thick blanket.* This helps dampen the paper.
- *Sponge and plant sprayer.* These are used to dampen dry sheets.
- *Small stiff-bristled brush.* This is helpful for coaxing the dampened paper into tight areas of rigid embossing materials.

Louise Schmidtzinsky uses unmounted rubber stamps to wet-emboss her handmade papers. The card shown at right is a collaboration between Louise, who created the embossed Egyptian queen featured on this card, and Lea Everse, who did the beautiful calligraphy, stamping, thermography, embossing, and spray web designs seen on the card and envelope.

- *Paper press or heavy weights.* If you don't have a paper press, bricks or jugs of water can be used. They should remain in place until your paper is dry. A dry-mount press is very useful, as it can apply pressure and drying heat at the same time. Some artists simply skip all of this equipment, however, and just drive their cars over a sandwich of boards, embossing materials, and paper. (They impress their papers and their friends at the same time.)

To emboss wet papers, place your embossing materials on a waterproofed press board, then lay your pressed handmade paper or dampened paper on top of the materials, right side up. Cover the paper with a dampened felt or blanket, top with a second press board, and apply pressure. Leave the embossing materials in place until the paper is dry. The embossing paper will stretch over the materials and then shrink around them as it dries, imparting texture and pattern to the paper.

Jean Marvell, who creates highly textured handmade sheets, uses another wet-embossing method that seems to work well. She places dry sheets of handmade paper over a textured surface and then, using a soft flat hake brush, dampens and strengthens the papers by painting them generously with methyl cellulose. She uses a small wad of dampened cheesecloth to press the paper into the textured areas of low-relief pieces, and often employs a firm stencil brush to help press the paper into forms with cutouts. When embossing a freshly made sheet of paper, Jean omits the top press board and instead uses a rolling pin to press water out of and press texture into the paper.

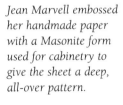

Jean Marvell embossed her handmade paper with a Masonite form used for cabinetry to give the sheet a deep, all-over pattern.

DRY EMBOSSING

To create an embossed design on a dry sheet of paper, you'll need:

- *A pencil.* This is used to draw the design to be embossed.
- *Tracing paper.* This is needed only if you decide to trace a design.
- *Two-ply plate-finish bristol board or lightweight mat board.* The embossing pattern can be cut from either of these materials. Scraps of these boards can also serve as mounting sheets.
- *X-Acto knife with #11 blade and self-healing cutting mat (or piece of glass with taped edges).* You'll need this equipment to cut the design to be embossed. Cutting curves will be easier if you invest in a swivel knife, too.
- *Glue stick or white glue.* You'll need glue to attach the embossing design to its mounting sheet.
- *Removable tape.* This holds your paper in place as it's being burnished.
- *Ball-tipped burnisher.* Although a bone folder can be used for some embossing, a ball-tipped burnisher, available at craft supply stores, allows you to do more detailed embossing.
- *Light source.* A good light source is critical to dry embossing. The embossing pattern must be illuminated from behind to define its edges so that you can run the ball burnisher against them. Invest in a light box if you can. You can also emboss by taping your design to a sunny window, or make a substitute light box by elevating a piece of glass or Plexiglas with wood blocks and placing a fluorescent bulb behind it.
- *Paper.* This is the last but most important material for dry embossing. Rag paper works well, as it will bend rather than tear or crack when you work on it. Art papers such as Strathmore, Ingres, Fabriano, and Rives, or your own handmade papers can all be embossed. White and light-colored papers are easiest to use. It's really difficult to see an embossing pattern through a dark paper. Then, too, because part of the beauty of an embossed design is the way light and shadow play on the raised surface, white paper is usually the best choice.

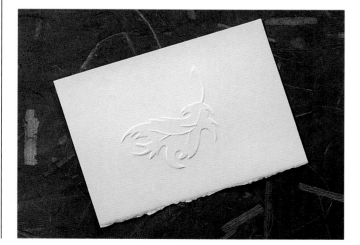

Edie Roberts's work exemplifies the best in dry embossing. Edie prefers to work on white paper, letting the interplay between light and shadow define the image.

Choosing and Cutting an Embossing Pattern

Choose a simple design from source material like a magazine, greeting card, or stencil book, or use your own design. Bear in mind that a silhouetted design with straight edges such as a triangle or a star will be easy to cut with an X-Acto knife, while intricate curved designs may require a swivel knife.

Draw or trace the design onto the center of a small piece of bristol or mat board. Place your board on a cutting mat and use your knife to cut out the design. Work slowly and carefully, using a fresh blade to avoid leaving ragged edges. The positive cut-out (a rabbit, for example) and the board from which it was removed (which now bears the negative shape of a rabbit) can both be used as embossing patterns.

Work slowly and carefully to cut out the embossing shape. Any ragged cutting will show up in your embossed design.

Move the embossing tool around the edge of the cut-out until a crisp image appears.

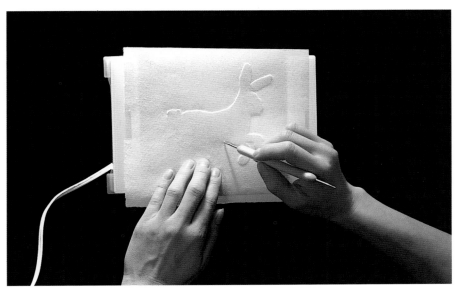

Embossing with a Positive Image

Use a spot of glue to join your cut-out to another piece of bristol board. Use removable tape to tape your embossing paper in place over the cut-out. Then move your mounted pattern and paper to a light box or hold them against a sunny window.

To begin embossing, first depress the area around the cut-out with your finger to outline the shape to be embossed. Then slowly move the wide end of a ball burnisher around the edge of the cut-out until a crisp pattern appears. Apply a minimum of pressure to avoid tearing the paper and turn the pattern as you work to reach all parts of the design. Be sure to leave the paper in place until you've completely embossed it. It's next to impossible to get it back in position once you've moved it.

Some papers tend to become shiny from being embossed. If that's a problem, try placing a piece of tracing paper between your tool and the paper you're embossing. Papers with a tooth or texture will sometimes cause the embossing tool to hesitate or drag. You can remedy this by rubbing the burnisher on a piece of waxed paper for a moment. The wax usually lubricates it and makes it glide more easily.

One advantage of embossing with the positive image is that it lets you mount several patterns on a single board and emboss a suite of images. Working with a positive image also allows you to emboss semi-flat objects, like string held beneath the paper, and even emboss cut-outs stacked on top of each other to create more dimensional designs. The beautiful work of Edie Roberts shows the range of images dry embossing can produce.

By working with positive cut-outs, Edie Roberts creates two-layer embossings.

Embossing with a Negative Image

The bristol board from which the cut-out was removed can also be used as a pattern to create a raised image. (In fact, embossing is easier this way.) NOTE: Because you're working with an inverted piece of paper, any images that must be read from left to right, like lettering, should be embossed in reverse.

Tape a sheet of paper right-side down over the opening in the board. Hold the board and paper over a light source and begin embossing as described above, this time pushing the edges of the paper down into the edge of the shaped opening. There's no need to emboss the interior of the cut-out; it will be lifted up by the embossed edges. When you've finished, untape the paper, flip it over and enjoy the raised image you've created. One advantage of embossing with a negative image is that because you're burnishing the back of the paper, there's no need to worry about paper shine.

Dreamweaver, a company in California, manufactures an array of brass stenciling/embossing plates with detailed designs that would be very difficult to cut by hand. Although nothing compares to making your own designs, these metal plates do allow you to raise finely detailed areas and add embossed calligraphy to handmade cards. You'll need a fine, blunt embossing tool to emboss through metal. You might also look for thin metal screens with decorative openings at yard sales. Sometimes old radiator covers have all-over repeat designs that create interesting embossed papers. The ready-made circles, squares, and curves in plastic drafting templates are also useful embossing plates.

Found and manufactured equipment for embossing a negative image includes metal stenciling and embossing plates, cut stencils, radiator screens, and drafting templates.

Traditional Stenciling

Traditional stenciling is a method of decorating paper or other materials by applying color through an opening cut in heavy paper or acetate. Embossing patterns with cut-out areas can often be adapted for stenciling. If you want to start from scratch, however, you'll need the following:

- *Stencil acetate.* Available in many sewing and craft supply shops, stencil acetate is the easiest material to begin stenciling with. It cuts easily and is translucent, allowing you to trace images from source material directly on it.
- *A pencil.* This is used to draw or trace designs onto the acetate.
- *X-Acto knife.* An X-Acto knife with a #11 blade and a swivel knife (optional) can be used to cut the stencil.
- *Cutting surface.* Either a self-healing cutting mat or a piece of glass with its edges taped can serve this purpose.
- *Removable tape.* Tape is needed to hold the stencil in place as color is applied to the paper.

Some of the materials and equipment used in traditional stenciling.

- *Color applicators.* Stencil brushes with natural bristles cut to the same length or foam daubers can be used to apply color. For small, detailed areas, it's handy to have small color applicators. To begin, three brushes, 1/4 inch to 1 inch (0.6 to 2.5 cm) in diameter, would be good. To apply color to large openings, a 3-inch (7.6-cm) foam paint roller can be used.
- *Paper towels.* These are used to remove excess color from your brushes and stencils.
- *Paper.* Just about any paper that's not too absorbent can be stenciled. White and colored drawing papers give fine results. Stencil designs on handmade paper and previously decorated paper can be really exciting.
- *Stenciling colors.* Acrylic paints and oil- and water-based printing inks are all good coloring agents for stencils. Paints with a creamy rather than runny consistency are easiest to use. Paint sticks, which are paints in solid form (available at art and craft supply stores), work exceptionally well and eliminate the bleeding under the stencil that sometimes occurs with liquid colors.
- *Optional equipment.* Hole punches and scissors that cut decorative as well as straight lines can be used to cut symmetrical openings in folded stencil acetate. A hole punch can also be used to make registration marks to help you reposition a stencil. A ruler is helpful if you want to draw straight lines.

CHOOSING A STENCIL DESIGN

Although precut stencils and metal embossing plates are easy to use, it's more rewarding to cut your own stencil. Simple geometric designs are easy to draw. If you don't feel comfortable drawing designs, you can trace them from cards, magazines, and design books. You can combine images and easily enlarge or reduce them on a photocopy machine. Precut stencils can be valuable if they're examined to see how the *bridges*—the solid pieces of acetate that separate the elements of a design—help to accent and define a silhouette. Once you've studied a precut stencil, you can always alter it with your X-Acto knife to give it more personality.

CUTTING THE STENCIL

After you've traced or drawn a design on your acetate, use a sharp X-Acto knife to cut it out. Work slowly and carefully, applying even pressure for the length of each cut to prevent jagged lines. Leave bridges between areas of a complicated design so that different colors may be applied and the negative space left by the bridge (which remains uncolored) can help define the image. If your stencil has several parts, cut the smaller areas first. Cutting out large areas weakens the stencil and makes fine cutting more difficult.

For a complicated design, or one that requires the addition of several colors, you may want to prick or punch small registration holes in the four outer corners of your stencil acetate. Marking your paper through these holes will allow you to remove the stencil and place it in position again. These registration marks can also be used as guides for positioning and duplicated on other stencils when superimposing one stenciled image over another.

APPLYING COLOR

Begin by taping your cut stencil in position over your paper. To charge your brush or dauber with color, hold it perpendicular and just touch the surface of the paint container with the flat edge of the applicator. Then, still holding your brush perpendicular, tap it against a paper towel or piece of scrap paper to distribute the color evenly. The brush or dauber should be almost dry when it's used; this keeps the color from bleeding under the stencil openings and blurring the edges of your designs. Loading your color applicator with the correct amount of color will come with experience. Proceed cautiously at first: You can always go over an area to darken it, but the paint can't be removed once it's applied.

Two methods of applying stencil paint include *stippling,* or tapping the perpendicular brush on the stencil opening, and *rouging,* which is done by moving an almost dry brush or dauber in a circular motion, rubbing the paint into the stencil openings. Work on top of the acetate at first, moving from the edge of the opening to its center, laying down a thin layer of color. If you're using a paint stick, follow the directions and deposit some color on waxed paper before picking it up with your brush or dauber. When using a roller, make sure it's almost dry before you start and apply a minimum of pressure.

It's not necessary to fill in the entire stencil opening with intense color. Sometimes a darker shading on the edges of the opening that leads to a lighter concentration of color in the center of a design, such as a flower, can be very effective. Filling a stencil opening with shades or tints of a color can also work nicely.

FINISHING

When you've finished applying color through your stencil, remove the tape and pick the stencil straight up so as not to smudge the stenciled design. Be sure to thoroughly wipe off any color on the stencil before it dries. If you're doing repeat patterns, be sure that the stencils are totally clean before moving them to another position on your paper. Be sure to clean your color applicators, too, so you don't have any surprise color mixtures when you stencil again.

Put your finished paper in a safe place to dry. (Designs stenciled with oil-based paints sometimes need to dry for several hours.)

Leave bridges, or uncut areas, between parts of a stencil to help define the image.

To apply color evenly through a stencil opening, work on the surrounding acetate at first, then move toward the opening's center.

Nontraditional Stenciling

Paper can also be decorated by using found stencils. Any number of objects with openings in them can be used as stencils. Plastic berry baskets, metal radiator screens, lace paper, doilies, rubber nonskid rug backings, metal grids for barbecuing fish, even a plastic fly swatter (new, of course) can yield interesting patterns for decorating paper. To begin you'll need:

- *Found stencil pattern.* Finding this is fun. Go on a treasure hunt and use your imagination.
- *Paper.* Most any type of paper will be fine for this type of stenciling. You'll also need newspaper to protect surfaces from paint overspray and to remove excess color from brush applicators.
- *Colors.* Acrylic paints in spray cans and jars and watercolor paints and dyes can be used for nontraditional stenciling.
- *Color applicators.* If you have access to an airbrush you can use it to spray paint through the openings of the found stencil. Next best are cans of acrylic spray paint. If you can stand the fumes, Krylon works great. (Work outside if possible, or wear a respirator.) Another useful tool is a mouth atomizer. The lowest of low-tech color applicators, a tongue depressor or ruler rubbed against a natural-bristle vegetable brush, spatters rather than sprays paint through the stencil openings, but the result looks good. (Of course, spattering paper without a stencil is also an effective means of decorating a sheet of paper or preparing a surface for stenciling or another paper decorating technique.)
- *Optional equipment.* A cardboard box is useful to catch the inevitable overspray from spattering. Remove the lid and the side closest to you, then place your paper in the box.

Claudia Lee sometimes sprays color through a found stencil to decorate her handmade paper stationery.

APPLYING COLOR

Apply color sparingly to avoid dripping paint. Hold the can of acrylic spray about 18 inches (45.7 cm) from the stencil and paper, propping them up vertically if necessary, then laying them flat after spraying to avoid paint drips. Practice using short bursts of paint, moving the can as you work to get the kind of light paint coverage necessary. You should be able to see a trace of the paper through the final spray.

To apply color with a vegetable brush and tongue depressor, coat the brush with color (acrylic works well) and tap off some of the paint on a piece of newspaper. Hold the brush bristles up, tilt the front of it slightly downward, and draw the tongue depressor *toward* you, spattering paint on your paper. Move your hands around as you work to deliver an even coat of paint. If you get large drips of paint, you probably need to work with less paint on your brush. Vary the intensity of the spatters by working closer to or farther away from the paper. This will help you get a feel for the technique. Because you'll no doubt spatter paint beyond your paper, you may want to work outside or place your paper in a cardboard box to spatter it.

When your first coat of paint is dry, try moving the found stencil to another position on your paper and spraying or spattering with another color. Shades of the same color or different colors can be used.

Spattering paper with acrylic paint while using a non-skid rug backing as a stencil.

STENCIL RESISTS

Another form of stenciling uses paper cut-outs, leaves, and found objects such as buttons, plastic slide mounts, paper clips, and washers to prevent paint from reaching parts of the paper. The negative or uncolored space is what forms the decorative design. A common type of stencil-resist pattern can be made by flattening leaves and distributing them on a sheet of paper to be spattered. Quite sophisticated designs can also be created with torn pieces of masking tape, such as "Music Screen" by Arlene Spurgin (below). Try cutting masking materials to produce more hard-edged designs.

"Music Screen" by Arlene Spurgin, 8 × 13 inches (20.3 × 33 cm). Arlene created this piece by tearing pieces of masking tape and applying them to watercolor paper. She sprayed on a light coat of acrylic paint, let it dry, and then moved the tape to another position before spraying again with another shade of paint. Many thin coats of paint were applied and the stencils moved many times to achieve the rich colors and patterns.

Lynell Harlow created this card by spattering paint around leaves, then adding a light spattered coat of paint over the negative areas formed by the leaves. A metal stenciling plate and embossing powder were used to create the sun.

Stamping

Although stamps are still used for many business purposes—for example, to identify or authenticate documents like passports—they're also used to decorate stationery, produce distinctive patterned papers, and create fine art. Several hundred stamp clubs exist in the United States alone, where new stamping techniques are constantly being explored.

Stamping can also be used to produce a type of embossing similar to the raised lettering seen on business cards. *Thermal embossing,* which is discussed on page 55, is done by sprinkling embossing powder on a wet inked image. When heat is applied, the powder melts, expands, and dries in a raised position.

To begin your own exploration of stamping, you'll need:

The various repeat patterns Ruth Ann Petree stamps on her handmade boxes gives each one a distinct personality.

- *Rubber stamp.* A purchased stamp, one you've created yourself (see "Creating Your Own Stamp," page 51), or one you've had laser-cut from an original design can all be used.
- *Rubber stamp inks.* Raised stamp pads in a range of solid, metallic, and rainbow colors and water-based brush markers are great to use. The markers are wonderful for creating color blends. Buy a set, if possible.
- *Paper.* You can stamp on most any paper, from brown wrapping paper to your own handmade paper. Some unsized papers stamped with water-based inks will yield beautiful, soft-edged designs.

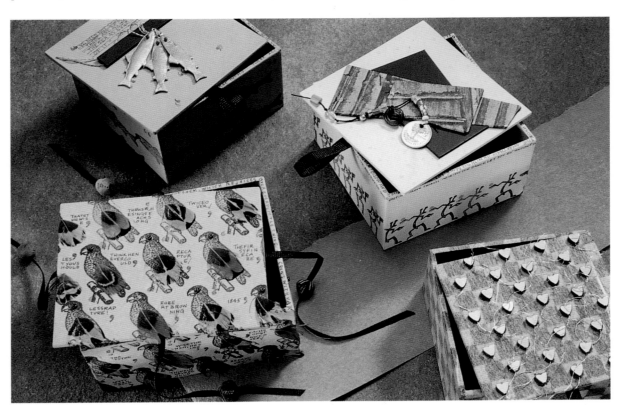

If you want to create your own stamp (see opposite), you'll also need the following:

- *Eraser.* A Mars-Staedtler Plastic Grand Eraser, Pink Pearl, or an other large eraser can be carved most easily.
- *Carving tools.* An X-Acto knife with #11 blades, a linoleum cutter with various sizes of V-blades, and a weaving needle or awl make good carving tools. You'll no doubt discover other makeshift tools as you begin carving. A friend swears by her broken-off car aerial for making certain designs; Mick Mather, who publishes a charming newsletter called *Eraser Carvers Quarterly,* suggests wheedling a set of old teeth-cleaning tools from your dentist. (Why not go for the drill, too?)
- *A pencil.* A soft pencil is useful for drawing designs on the eraser or tracing designs from other sources.
- *Tracing paper.* This is used for working out original designs and for transferring designs to an eraser.
- *Optional equipment.* A ruler may come in handy. An alcohol-soaked cotton ball can be used to remove printed logos from erasers and transfer photocopied images from source material.

Additional equipment needed for thermal embossing is discussed on page 55.

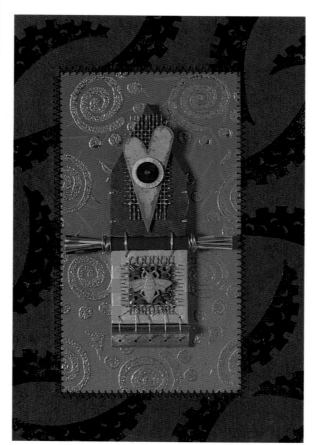

Betsy Veness often applies embossing powder over a rubber-stamped image to create a background for her collage work.

CREATING YOUR OWN STAMP

Creating rubber stamp art is doubly rewarding when you design and cut your own stamp. Start out with a simple pattern stamp at first, them move on to more elaborate designs.

Choosing a Design

The first step in carving your own stamp is choosing and transferring a design to your eraser. Clip-art books, illustrations from magazines and newspapers, computer-generated drawings, or your own drawings can all become stamp designs. Studying wrapping paper and fabric designs can often yield ideas for pattern stamps. A series of dots, lines, and randomly gouged patterns are easy to carve but create quite sophisticated textural designs when repeatedly stamped side by side or over each other slightly out of register.

Transferring the Design

Use alcohol and a cotton ball to remove any printed logo from the eraser and cut the eraser to an appropriate size. Then use a pencil (and ruler, too, if making straight lines) to draw directly on your eraser, bearing in mind that what you draw will print in reverse. If you trace a design from source material or work out your own drawing on tracing paper you can invert your tracing onto the eraser and rub the back of the image with your fingernail or a coin to transfer it to the eraser.

Images can be photocopied to enlarge or reduce them and then transferred to an eraser. Just lay the photocopy face down on the eraser and rub the back of it with a cotton ball soaked in alcohol to transfer the design. Touch up the design with a pencil or pen if necessary.

Carving a Sketched Design

Once you have well-defined lines to follow, it's time to begin cutting away the unwanted material around your design. Always make sure you cut away from your design so there's enough eraser remaining under it to support it for repeated stamping. Work slowly, inking and stamping as you cut to make sure you're cutting deeply enough and removing the parts you intend to. Remember, you can always make another cut, but you can't reattach eraser parts removed in error. (I learned this one creating my exotic three-legged pig stamp.)

Push the V-shaped linoleum cutter away from you to remove parts of the eraser, remembering to keep the printing surface level. The X-Acto knife is handy for cutting fine detailed areas and trimming away borders. Use the awl to create holes or scratch away parts of the eraser to create fine lines.

After transferring or drawing an image on your eraser, begin cutting away the unwanted portions.

Cutting Free-form Patterns

Many stamps with images that resemble textures or patterns can be cut without first drawing designs on them. A series of dots, intersecting lines, and designs that resemble pebbles or scattered leaves are easy to create. Because only small amounts of eraser material are removed, undercutting is not a concern. With pattern stamps, a series of intersecting lines, for instance, will form a negative image, allowing the paper color to show through.

The inked part of the eraser stamp (the positive image) will be the area around the lines. When cutting a stamp designed for repeat patterns, trim away as much of the stamp border as possible to allow images to be stamped close to each other.

MODIFYING PURCHASED STAMPS

Although there are thousands of great ready-made stamps available (even some that utter barnyard sounds when you use them), many people feel uncomfortable, even a little guilty, using a design that they didn't personally create. Then, too, sometimes you'll find a manufactured stamp that would be a really terrific accent for a project if only it didn't have the cutesy hearts on it.

In either case, modifying the stamp can solve the problem. I once found a stamp depicting a paper cutter that I then modified to preserve the fine grid of its base only. It's a great pattern stamp now. I amputated the postage meter mark from another stamp, leaving fine parallel wavy lines that would be very time-consuming to cut.

LASER-CUT DESIGNS

Your own artwork, even rather detailed designs, can be laser-cut and made into a rubber stamp. Check your local telephone directory for a shop that specializes in making rubber stamps. Although they are a bit pricey because the designs are usually sent off to be cut, the stamp detail is great, lots of time is saved, and the design is an original.

INKING THE STAMP

Stamp pads come in various colors, metallics, and rainbow designs. The rainbow pads have several bands of color in one pad, so that you can print multicolored designs. To use a stamp pad, merely press your stamp against it with enough force to deposit ink on the relief design. If you press too hard, though, you'll ink the background of the stamp (or even the wood block it's attached to, if you're using a purchased stamp).

Another type of stamp pad is about 1 inch (2.5 cm) square with a raised, inked sponge surface. To use one, just press it against the stamp to deposit ink. These raised pads also come in a larger format for inking large stamps.

My favorite tools for applying color to rubber stamps are watercolor brush pens. Parts of the stamp can be inked in different colors, and color blends can also be created. One drawback, however, is that sometimes people get so involved with creating the perfect color blend on their stamp that parts of it can begin to dry. By exhaling onto your stamp just before using it, you can usually remoisten drying areas. Because metallic markers and some opaque pigment inks tend to dry more slowly, you can use them at a more leisurely pace.

Watercolor brush pens allow you to ink your stamp with more than one color and create color blends. The swallow stamp was laser-cut from a design drawn by Jeff Mathison.

STAMPING REPEATS

To begin stamping, press your inked stamp against your paper firmly, without rocking it. Re-ink the stamp about every third stamping to create images that fade in and out. Rotate the stamp 90 or 180 degrees to create other variations in a repetitive design. Interesting border designs for stationery and matching envelopes can be made by alternating stamp designs or by stamping in one color and then restamping over the initial image in a related color, with a lighter value, allowing the images to overlap slightly. Horizontal repeat patterns that resemble the way bricks line up or half-drop repeat patterns running in a vertical direction can also yield interesting patterned papers.

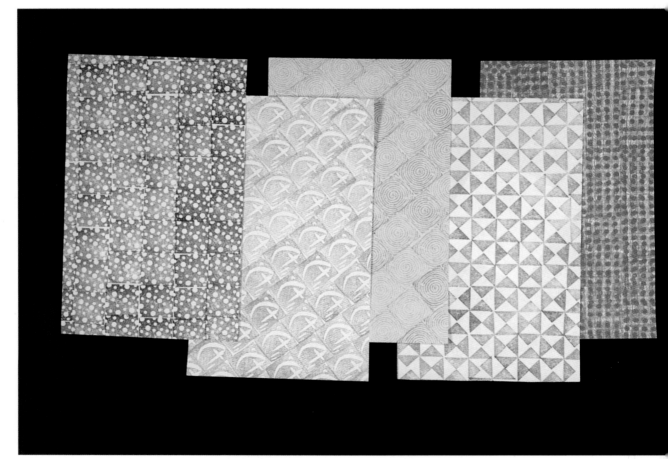

Although pattern stamps are easy to cut, they can be used to create quite sophisticated repeat designs. These stamped papers are by Katherine McKearn. Katherine created the first paper by pressing antenna tubes into an eraser and then excising the plugs that remained. Papers two and three were made by carving erasers in a conventional manner. The fourth paper was made by cutting diagonal lines across a square eraser and slicing out alternating triangles. The fifth paper was made by stamping several pattern stamps over each other to create a multiple-image design.

To create a sheet of decorative paper with lots of dimension, try stamping an all-over repeat design (sometimes called a *diaper pattern*) with a pattern stamp. When the sheet is dry, go back and stamp over the entire sheet with another pattern stamp using a related color. If designs are simple, sometimes a third and fourth image can be added as well, without the sheet becoming too busy.

For stamped images that look like they were made with watercolor paints, ink your stamp with water-based inks and then dampen it with a fine mist from a spray bottle before stamping.

THERMAL EMBOSSING

By applying embossing powder to a wet stamped image and then heating and melting the powder, you can create a raised glossy design similar to the commercial thermography designs seen on fine stationery and business cards. Embossing powders are available in many solid, metallic, and pearlescent colors. Clear embossing powder is also available to highlight colors stamped beneath them and give the stamped image a glossy wet look. The powders can be melted by holding the stamped and powdered sheet of paper over an iron or a light bulb, but these methods usually take a long time to melt the powder and sometimes scorch papers. It makes good sense to visit your local craft store to buy an embossing gun, which is specifically designed for melting embossing powders. It will make embossing much easier.

To emboss an image, first coat your stamp with a slow-drying ink. Clear inks are recommended if you plan to coat the image with a colored embossing powder. Stamp your image on the paper, then sprinkle the embossing powder over it. Shake the paper to spread the powder over the stamped image. Then shake the excess powder onto a piece of folded paper so that it can easily be returned to the bottle. Use a cotton swab or small brush to wipe away any powder that's clinging to parts of the paper you don't intend to emboss. Then heat the powder (from above, if using an embossing gun) to melt it and create the embossed image.

You can use watercolor brush markers to fill in the interior areas of an embossed image, creating color blends. If you get color on the embossed surface, just use a cotton swab to wipe it off. Fred B. Mullett, who creates sensational stamps from nature prints and amazing art from his stamps, is the undisputed master of stamp embossing and coloring techniques. He often uses a spot application of embossing powders to selected areas of a stamped image, a process that he says is "like painting with plastic." The photos on page 56 show Fred at work on one of his embossed fish paintings.

When you're through using a stamp or decide to switch ink color, be sure to stamp off excess ink, then clean the stamp with a damp towel or sponge to prevent surprise color mixtures from cropping up and ruining subsequent designs. Commercial stamp-cleaning pads may be necessary if you're using oil-based pigments.

(Near right) Fred B. Mullett inks an oversized rubber stamp with black and light gray inks blended together to create an even transition in value.

(Far right) After selectively applying the pink embossing powder with a straw, Fred applies black embossing powder to the top of the print. Clear powder is dusted over the remainder of the print to show the ink colors and values. Fred shakes the print to distribute the powder and remove any excess, then uses an embossing gun to melt the powder and raise the image.

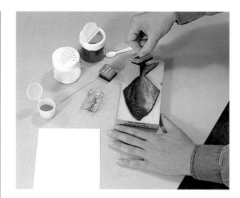

(Left) A single dark watercolor is applied to the top of the image and blended and faded downward, creating a sense of shape and depth. (It slides off the embossed areas and colors the paper around them.) After the watercolor dries, accents are added with colored markers.

Some of Fred Mullett's stamped and embossed images.

Vegetable Printing

A number of fruits and vegetables can be inked and applied to paper to create sophisticated or playful repeat designs. Onions, broccoli, apples, and citrus fruits can all be cut in half, dried on a paper towel, and inked to stamp mirror images of their cross sections. Potatoes and pumpkins can be carved and inked to create designs that look as though they were made from more rigid materials. Although the fine detail achieved with block prints (see page 61) can't be duplicated in a potato print, and the longevity of the vegetable block is limited (especially if you're cutting it at lunch time), the ease with which the vegetable block can be carved makes it fun to use.

To experiment with potato printing, you'll need:

- *A potato.* Any kind or size of potato will do.
- *Carving tools.* A small sharp kitchen knife, a vegetable peeler, nails, and other sharp objects can be used to cut and score the potato.
- *Paper towels.* These help remove excess moisture from potatoes.
- *Colors.* Acrylic and watercolor paints and foam stamp pads can be used. Watercolor brush pens also work fine as long as the surface of the potato isn't too wet.
- *Brushes.* Small, soft watercolor brushes are used to coat the potato with paint. You can omit them if you use brush pens.
- *Paper.* Most any type of paper can be used for potato printing. Scrap paper can be used to test block-cutting progress and paint or ink coverage and to protect tabletops.

Some of the materials and equipment used for vegetable printing.

CARVING THE POTATO

To prepare a printing block with a flat surface, use a sharp knife to slice off a 1-inch-thick (2.5-cm-thick) chunk of potato. Use a nail, if necessary, to scratch out a simple design like a square, triangle, or rectangle. If you want more variation, cut notches into the sides of these simple shapes. Cut away the areas around your design so that the entire potato block assumes the shape you've drawn. Designs carved in relief, which use the rest of the potato as a handle, don't allow you to space designs close together. By carving away everything but the printing shape, you can easily create tight repeat designs and place the images exactly where you want them.

To create textured or patterned printing blocks, use a knife to score parts of the potato. Parts of the interior of the potato block can also be removed by digging out areas with the tip of a knife, a nail, or a vegetable peeler.

INKING THE POTATO

Begin by pressing the potato block against a paper towel to remove some of the moisture. Let the potato stand for about a 1/2 hour to dry it out a bit. Then brush color onto the block. Begin printing with solid colors at first. Later you can create stripes and color blends by coating the block with several brushes or markers. It's fun to start out with three different potato blocks and ink each with a different shade of the same color or another harmonious color. If you need to change colors using the same block, simply print it dry, wipe it with a damp paper towel, and re-ink it. This works best when you print light colors first. Because the potato absorbs some of the ink, going from a dark color to a pale one may pose problems.

MAKING THE PRINT

When the potato is coated with color, press it against the paper to make a print. (You may want to make a test print on a piece of scrap paper first, to see if you want to use more or less ink to create a particular effect.) Lift the potato straight up after printing so you don't smear the design. Play with patterning suggestions mentioned earlier, then raid the vegetable bin to turn up other printing tools.

After the potato stamp has dried for about a 1/2 hour, you can begin coating it with color and making prints.

Printing with Found Objects

Objects with relatively flat textured surfaces can be used to create some unusual decorative "junk print" papers. Hardware stores, garage sales, and kitchen catchall drawers are good places to begin the treasure hunt for novel printing devices. Small objects like antique coins, washers, nuts, and other machine parts can be pressed into a stamp pad and then used to print a sheet of paper. Larger objects, such as embossed cookie tin lids, carved boxes, wire mesh, bicycle pedals, gears, and kitchen implements, require more equipment. To ink and print larger objects, you'll need:

- *Plexiglas or glass inking tile.* This is used as a spreading surface for the ink.
- *Brayer or roller.* A roller is used to spread the ink on the inking surface and roll it onto the printing object. Foam poly brushes will also come in handy for inking parts of an object that are difficult to reach with a roller.
- *Colors.* Acrylic paints and water- or oil-based block-printing inks, which are thicker-bodied and slower-drying than rubber-stamp inks, can coat an entire object very efficiently. They can be obtained at art supply stores.
- *Paper.* Block-printing papers, handmade papers, and certain brands of Japanese papers, such as Hosho, Moriki, and Okawara, will produce the best images. There are also many white and colored drawing papers that print well. Experiment to find your favorite.
- *Newspapers.* Newspapers are needed to cover tabletops, absorb excess color, and create a padded printing surface when necessary.

Odd objects residing in a catch-all drawer can be used to make interesting "junk prints."

- *Gloves or barrier hand cream.* If you're working with acrylic paints or water-based inks, latex gloves are recommended to prevent stained hands. Heavier rubber gloves are more appropriate for oil-based inks, which require the use of toxic thinners. If you would rather not wear gloves, you can apply a barrier hand cream, which is made in both water- and oil-repellant formulations and can be purchased at art supply stores and some pharmacies.
- *Cleanup equipment.* Sponges, rags, and solvents may be necessary, depending upon what types of inks you use.

Squeeze out several inches of tube paint or teaspoons of ink onto the inking tile. Use the brayer to evenly spread the ink by rolling it in horizontal, vertical, and diagonal directions. When the brayer is coated, roll it over the surface of the object you're printing to evenly disperse the ink. Then press the inked object against the paper to print it. Some heavy rigid objects, like metal tools, print better if they're pressed against a padded surface. If an object isn't leaving a good impression, try placing your paper on top of a newspaper pad before making another print. Make several prints to determine how much ink is required to produce a satisfactory image. Try repeatedly printing with one object or combine printed images on one sheet of paper.

Tubular found objects, like patterned lipstick tubes, cut-glass jars, and the caps from products like glue sticks or coffee jars, can be rolled onto the inking surface and then onto the printing paper.

Small, flat found objects of the same thickness can be grouped together and glued to a wooden base to form a printing block. Pieces of smooth and corrugated cardboard, string, netting, keys, pieces of rubber, puzzle pieces, and a range of other objects, can create interesting prints. Be sure to glue the pieces down with waterproof glue and coat them with urethane to reuse the printing block.

Inking part of a pastry tool to use as a printing device.

Printing with Carved Blocks

Foamcore board, balsa wood, soft linoleum, and Safety-Kut, a new block-print material, can be carved to produce a relief design or patterned surface. Unlike harder materials such as battleship linoleum and wood, which require carving gouges and a good deal of elbow grease, the softer materials can be cut with ease. Abstract designs can be made by nicking and scoring the surface of the block. More detailed works can be made by drawing or tracing a design onto a block, penciling in the areas you want to print, and using linoleum carving tools or an X-Acto knife to carve away the others. If you're doing complicated designs, be sure to ink your block and print as you carve so that you can monitor your progress. Remember—especially if carving a letterform—that you'll be printing a mirror image of the design.

If you're creating a block to be used in a repeat pattern, make a small notch at the edge of block to help position it within a series of images. You may also want to rule pencil or chalk lines to guide placement of the block, or you could print by eye, and allow the slight imperfections to lend character to the print.

For large detailed blocks carved from harder materials, the best print is often achieved by placing a soft printmaking paper over the inked block and applying pressure to the paper with a bone folder, wooden spoon, or soft rubber roller, which can more easily push the paper down into the block so the whole image prints. If you still have difficulty getting a good print, you may need to apply more pressure. Try putting a heavy board over the paper and block and then standing on it for a moment.

"Yellow Chair," a block print by Mary Mark, 15 × 17 inches (38.1 × 43.2 cm). Both the print and the lino block from which it was made are framed together in this work.

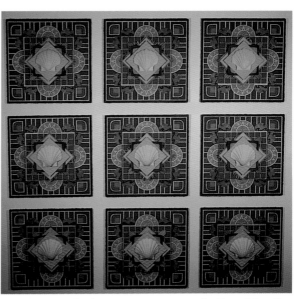

"Deco L'Image," a lino-cut repeat pattern by Betsy Miraglia, 50 × 50 inches (127 × 127 cm). Rubber stamping and cast paper are also used in this piece.

Printing with Rollers

Rollers or brayers can be loaded on an inking tile and then used directly on paper to create prints. Beautiful split-fountain color blends can be created by rolling out a band of color and then depositing a second band of color so that it overlaps the first one slightly. The bands can run parallel to each other or be angled away from each other so that only parts of them intersect. To create patterns that fade in and out, continue rolling without re-inking as the roller dries.

Create patterned bands of color by incising or carving away parts of rollers. Multiple-image roller prints can be made by coating a carved roller with a different color ink and rolling it over the first print in the same or opposite direction. The roller surface can also be built up. Glue on pieces of string, foam, or felt, or apply pieces of self-adhesive Buttercut (see page 26).

A print by Jeff Mathison. Jeff used a roller that was just barely inked and added stamped accents to the work.

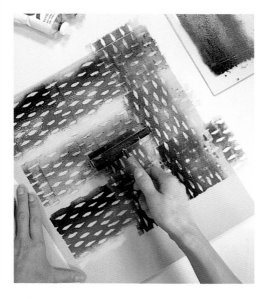

Printing with a carved roller. Color blends can be created by placing small amounts of ink on the inking tile and rolling the brayer over them to spread and mix them.

Rorschach Printing

Another printing technique that conjures up images of grade school is the symmetrical Rorschach inkblot, long used for psychological testing. I might not have even included examples of it in this book if Carin Quinn hadn't sent me her stunning prints, which amazed me. If you've only done the Rorschach technique with black inks, try using vibrant colored and metallic acrylics. Materials and equipment are minimal. You'll need:

- *Paper.* Smooth, light coverstock and lighter-weight papers in black, white, and colors can be used.
- *Colors.* All varieties of paints and inks will work, but acrylics produce especially dramatic results.
- *Brayer (optional).* You can use either a brayer or your hands to spread the paint or ink within the folded paper.
- *An iron.* After the print has dried, an iron is used to eliminate the fold from its center.

Fold a sheet of paper in half. Then open it out and squeeze or drop various colored inks or paints into the crease of the fold. Add paints on top of or beside each other. Apply colors at random or consider the color blends that will be created when the colors mix with each other. Then refold the paper and apply pressure using your hands or a brayer to rub away from the fold in all directions. Rub up and down along the fold line, too. Then open the paper and allow it to dry before pressing it with an iron, if necessary, to minimize the fold.

The printed image is always something of a surprise, but some control can be exercised by choosing where to apply the paint, how much paint to use, and how much pressure to exert when spreading the paint. You can also add colors a little at a time, then rub or roll over the paper each time.

(Below left) After distributing the paint by rolling over the folded paper, open the sheet. If you're not satisfied with the print, add more paint, refold the sheet and roll over it again. (Below right) An acrylic Rorschach print by Carin Quinn. Image size is 11 × 8½ inches (27.9 × 21.6 cm).

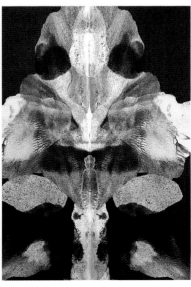

Ink-Blown Prints

Ink-blowing is another simple technique that can produce sophisticated images. You'll need the following materials and equipment:

- *Paper.* Various Oriental and Western papers will yield different types of images, so experiment with papers from both categories.
- *Colors.* Drawing inks or very liquid water-based colors can be used.
- *Propellants.* Although a soda straw can be used to blow inks into plantlike structures, an air-mist bottle from an art supply store or a canned-air dust remover from a camera shop propels inks further, faster, and with more pizzazz.

Deposit small drops of the same or different colored inks on a sheet of paper. Start with just a few drops so you can propel them before they are absorbed by the paper. Place the propellant close to each ink drop and blow it into a design, letting different colored inks mix with each other. Adjust the position of the propellant to blow at the inks from different angles. Blow the ink from overhead to create images that look like exploding fireworks; blow it sideways to create great sea forms with spiky tendrils. Layer images over each other to create highly textured designs. If you want soft-edged designs, work on more absorbent paper or dampen your paper before printing. (NOTE: Be sure to hold the propellant can upright and follow the manufacturer's directions to avoid skin burns.)

Using a can of air to blow inks into a design.

"Keepers" by Rona Chumbook, 11 × 14 inches (27.9 × 35.6 cm). Collage and art-stamping with ink-blowing and plastic-wrap printing (see opposite). After placing rinsed seaweed on misted watercolor paper to begin this work, Rona poured and squirted calligraphy inks and opaque acrylics close to the seaweed and surrounding areas. She then sprayed canned air on top of the pooled colors to achieve the spiky ink-blown effect.

Plastic-Wrap Prints

Plastic wrap can be applied to paper that has been coated with inks or diluted paints to produce various textured patterns. To try this type of printing, you'll need:

- *Paper.* Medium to heavy watercolor paper is ideal. I like to use a *watercolor block,* which is a stack of paper bound on four sides in order to hold wet paper flat until you pry it free with a dull knife. Plastic-wrap printing makes the paper very wet, so that it tends to buckle as it dries. Regular watercolor paper can be used, but you may have to dampen and stretch the paper before using it (see "Paper-stretching equipment," below).
- *Colors.* Drawing inks and thinned watercolors or acrylics are all good choices.
- *Color applicators.* If your inks don't come with squeeze-top applicators or if you use paints instead, you can squirt colors onto the paper with eyedroppers or pipettes. Large watercolor brushes or foam brushes can also be used to apply and distribute paint.
- *Spray bottle.* If your colors begin to dry out as you're working, misting the paper with water will help keep them runny and can also help move colors around.
- *Paper-stretching equipment (optional).* If you're not using a watercolor block, you may want to wet your paper and stretch it by stapling it to a sheet of plywood before applying colors. That way the paper will be held taut and your plastic-wrap print will dry flat instead of buckled. (Some lighter-weight papers can be printed and later pressed flat enough for use in various projects.)
- *Gloves (optional).* You may want to wear latex exam gloves to protect your hands from inks.

Squirting ink under the crumpled plastic wrap to create color mixtures. The plastic can be repositioned to create a tighter or looser fractured design.

Squirt or brush colored inks or diluted paints on the surface of your paper. The colors should be quite liquid and forming puddles. Spray the colors with water to dilute them, if necessary, and move them around. You can also tilt your board or block of paper to encourage them to run in a particular direction or distribute them with a very wet foam brush. To produce a pattern that resembles ice or rock formations, crumple a sheet of plastic wrap in a random manner and place it over the wet colors. While the colors are still wet, you can rearrange the plastic and press down on it to force the colors into designs. You can also squirt colors under the plastic to create color mixtures. Pull the plastic wrap into long narrow bands to create patterns that look like rocky plateaus and landscapes. When you've finished arranging the plastic, weight it with a book or board to keep it in position until the inks dry.

A plastic-wrap print created with drawing inks on watercolor paper.

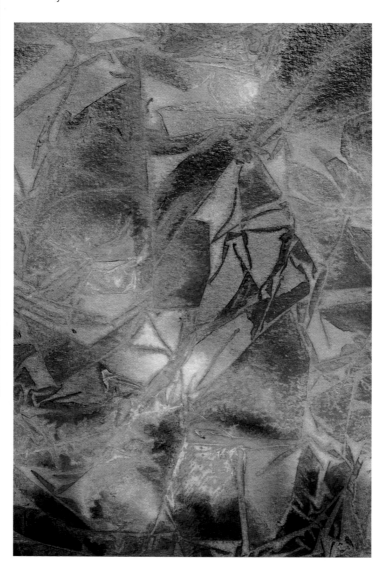

Salt Printing

If a very liquid color wash is brushed onto a paper and salt is applied while the color is still wet, the salt will wick the color around it to produce a mottled pattern as it dries. This technique, which is often used for painting on silk, is an equally effective method of patterning paper. To experiment with this technique, you'll need:

- *Paper.* A watercolor block or stretched watercolor paper is recommended to keep the wet paper from buckling as it dries. Other lighter-weight, nonabsorbent papers can be patterned with this technique and later pressed flat.
- *Colors.* Diluted watercolors, acrylic paints, or drawing inks can be used.
- *Color applicators.* Watercolor wash brushes or foam poly brushes are used to apply the color wash.
- *Salt.* Each type and grain size—table salt, kosher salt, even pretzel salt—will produce starburst patterns in different sizes.

Apply a wash of color to the paper, then immediately sprinkle on salt granules in either a random or controlled manner. The pattern is more interesting if the salt granules remain distinct and aren't clumped together. Let the color dry before brushing off the salt.

"Coral Reef" by Dorothy Grebos, 15 × 11 inches (38.1 × 27.9 cm). Salt printing with watercolors. The fish were created by using contact paper cut-outs to lift color from the work.

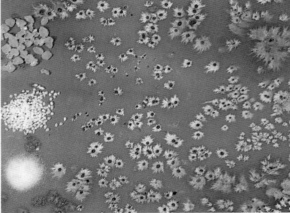

Ice cream salt, pretzel salt, and table salt attract and absorb wet drawing inks to form large and small starburst designs.

Leaf Printing

Once used by doctors and pharmacists to identify plants used in medicines, leaf prints are a great way to remember an exotic vacation or a particularly fine day in the woods. The detailed textures of tree and plant leaves, barely noticeable most of the time, can be faithfully reproduced in a leaf print. Once you begin foraging you'll probably find an unlimited supply of printing materials right in your own backyard, rooftop garden, or local park. You can press leaves for winter use or prune your houseplants if you live in a colder climate. Some houseplants, like my deer's foot fern, yield great prints without any pressing. To explore leaf printing, you'll need:

- *Leaves.* Look for living leaves with textured surfaces and veins running through them. Ferns, geranium leaves, maple, and ginkgo leaves are favorite printing subjects. Avoid smooth glossy leaves, as they usually print as a solid shape. Avoid poison oak and poison ivy, too.
- *Plant press.* Actually, a city phone directory will work just as well. It will help flatten the leaves and remove some of the moisture from them. Leave a few pages between specimens. If you live in a small town, your phone book may not be heavy enough, so add a few books to weight it down.
- *Sheet of Plexiglas.* This is your leaf-inking plate.
- *Colors.* Water-based, oil-based, and acrylic paints can all be used to coat the leaf. Ink pads and brush markers can also be used. Try ink pads and watercolors at first; you can easily mix colors and you'll avoid the extensive cleanup working with oils requires.
- *Color applicators.* Small watercolor brushes, foam stamp pads, and soft rubber rollers or brayers can be used to coat the leaf with color. The brushes can be used for color mixing, too. (If using oils, you'll probably also need a palette knife.)

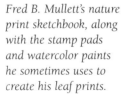

Fred B. Mullett's nature print sketchbook, along with the stamp pads and watercolor paints he sometimes uses to create his leaf prints.

- *Tweezers (optional).* These are helpful for picking up the inked leaf and placing it in position on the printing paper.
- *Paper.* Drawing paper, Oriental paper, watercolor paper, or Western printmaking paper will yield fine leaf prints. Inexpensive bond paper also works quite well.
- *Newspaper and scrap paper.* Newspapers can be used to protect working surfaces. Scrap paper protects your fingers from ink when making the print.

"Untitled" by Sonja Larsen, 19 × 12 inches (48.3 × 30.5 cm). Sonja first created a watercolor landscape on plastic, then transferred the image to paper. She then coated grass with oil paint and used it to print on top of the watercolor.

INKING THE LEAF

If you're working with a roller, place a small amount of water-based printer's ink on the Plexiglas and roll it out. Then carefully roll the inked brayer over the flattened leaf, depositing a thin, even layer of ink over its entire surface. Too much ink will cause your print to show fuzzy edges; too little ink will yield an incomplete image. Experiment to learn how much ink to apply.

If using watercolor paints or brush markers, coat the leaf as evenly as possible, creating color blends, if desired. If using a foam stamp pad, press the leaf against the pad; if it's a raised pad, press the pad against the leaf.

MAKING THE PRINT

Use the tweezers or your fingers to gently lift the leaf and deposit it, ink side down, on the printing paper. Then roll over it with a clean brayer or cover it with a piece of scrap paper and use your fingers to gently rub it down. When all parts of the leaf have made contact with the printing paper, lift the leaf up and set it aside to ink it again for another print.

You can make simultaneous prints of the front and the back of the leaf by rolling out ink on your Plexiglas, placing the leaf on top of the ink, face down, and rolling over the back of the leaf with the inked brayer. Then pick up the leaf with tweezers, place it on top of a piece of printing paper, and cover it with another sheet of printing paper. Gently rub the leaf through the top sheet of paper to create the double prints.

Creating a leaf print with a deer's foot fern, using watercolor markers and raised stamp pads.

Paste Papers

Paste papers are close relatives of the finger-painted papers that were so captivating in our youth and just as easy to make. The basic technique involves dampening a sheet of paper, coating it with colored paste, and then drawing various implements through the paste to displace it and create patterns. Kitchen tools, hairpicks, chopsticks, and lots of found objects can be used to make deceptively sophisticated designs. To begin paste paper adventures, you'll need the following equipment:

- *Paste.* Rice flour, wheat flour, cornstarch, and methyl cellulose can all be used to make paste (or starch) papers.
- *Additives.* Glycerin (available at pharmacies) and dish detergent are added to some flour paste formulas to keep them smooth and pliable and prevent cracking after drying.
- *A cooking pot.* A 2-quart (2.3-ml) saucepan will be fine for cooking up the paste.
- *Measuring cup and measuring spoons.* Use these to measure the ingredients for making the paste.
- *A large fine-mesh strainer.* Use this to strain the paste.

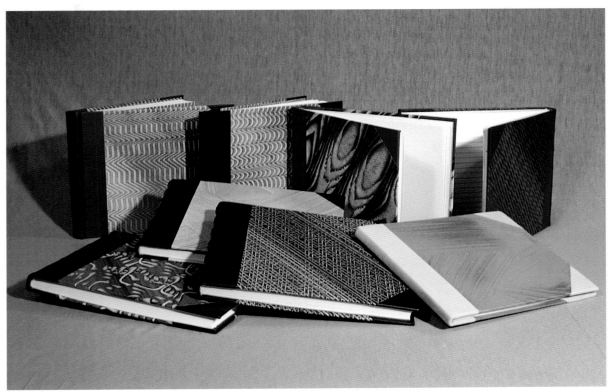

Paste-paper books by Susan Kristoferson. Images were made with an assortment of implements, including paint brushes and graining combs used to simulate wood.

- *Paints.* Many coloring agents can be used to make paste papers. Tube gouache and good brands of acrylic paint in tubes, like Golden or Liquitex, give excellent results. (Don't buy fluid acrylics, as they tend to dilute the paste too much.) Invest in a range of colors and be sure to include some metallics and pearlescent paints. Poster paints can also be used, but the colors aren't as intense.
- *Teaspoons.* These can be old garage sale items. They're used for stirring the paint into the prepared paste.
- *Gloves (optional).* Wear latex exam gloves to avoid staining your hands.
- *Colored paste containers.* Plastic food storage containers with snap-tight lids are ideal. They must be big enough to accommodate your paint brush. Empty tuna cans covered with plastic wrap are second best.
- *Brushes.* Several large 2- to 4-inch (5.1- to 10.2-cm) high-quality house-painting brushes are needed, one for each color. Don't skimp here—cheap brushes lose their bristles (usually in the middle of a design). Foam brushes can be used with thinner pastes.
- *Paper.* Most nonabsorbent medium-weight papers are fine for making paste designs. The paper must be strong enough to withstand having tools drawn across it in a dampened state without shredding. I use Canson Mi-Teintes, Strathmore, and Mohawk Superfine papers, but many offset printing papers also work fine. Get a supply of colored as well as white papers. Black papers are especially attractive when they're covered with a gold or silver paste design.

Some of the many tools that can be used to pattern paste papers. The paper shown was made by brushing paste on a sheet of paper, rolling over it with a soft brayer, then displacing the rolled paste with a calligraphy pen.

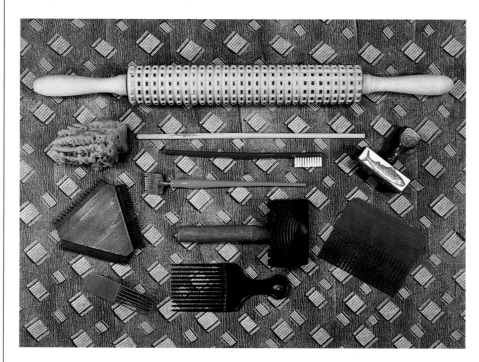

- *Large shallow tub.* A large plastic storage box filled with water is perfect for wetting your papers. You can also store your paste paper equipment in it between sessions. A nearby sink can also be used to wet your papers.
- *Work surface.* A piece of Plexiglas 3 inches (12.7 cm) larger on all sides than the paper you plan to pattern is a good investment. Alternatives include an old Formica or enamel tabletop or a flat work surface covered with plastic.
- *Sponges.* These will be used for wetting the paper, for making sponge prints in the paste, and for cleanup.
- *Small plastic water bucket.* This gives you a place to dip the sponge for cleanup and for sponging down the paper to be pasted.
- *Patterning tools.* Many household tools and found objects can be used to make paste papers. Forks, pastry wheels, buttons, and rolling pins with decorative designs, in addition to those noted earlier, are but a few of the many patterning tools you may already have on hand. Other great implements for making designs include woodgraining combs, multiple-line calligraphy pens, and potter's tools. Even corks, pieces of cardboard, and plastic milk cartons can be fashioned into paste-paper stamps and combs with assistance from an X-Acto knife or some scissors.

MAKING THE PASTE

Many paste-paper makers swear by a favorite recipe. We use the three recipes that follow. The flour paste is a bit stiffer and more granular in texture, while the cornstarch and methyl cellulose paste recipes yield smoother patterned papers.

Flour Paste. Measure 3 cups (750 ml) water; set aside. Blend 4 tablespoons (60 g) rice flour and 3 tablespoons (45 g) wheat flour in a saucepan with a little of the water. Add the remaining water and cook the mixture over medium heat, stirring constantly, until it resembles a thin custard. Remove the paste from the heat and stir in a $^1/_2$ teaspoon (2.5 ml) glycerin and 1 teaspoon (5 ml) dish detergent to keep the paste smooth and pliable. Let the paste cool and thicken before pushing it through a strainer to remove any lumps.

Cornstarch Paste. Mix a $^1/_4$ cup (62.5 ml) cornstarch with a $^1/_4$ cup (62.5 ml) water until well blended. Then add 1 cup (250 ml) water and heat the mixture while stirring until it resembles a thick custard. Finally, stir in a $^1/_2$ cup (125 ml) water to thin it down. Let the mixture cool and rethicken before using.

Methyl Cellulose Paste. Mix the paste according to package directions, which may vary among manufacturers. You want the paste to be about the consistency of toothpaste when you brush it on the papers.

COLORING THE PASTE

Divide the paste among several bowls. Start by adding about 2 to 3 teaspoons (10 to 15 ml) of color to a ¹/₂ cup (125 ml) of paste. Add paint gradually to achieve the desired color. Bear in mind that colored paste will dry on the paper a bit lighter than it looks in the container. If you want to darken a color slightly, add just a touch of black—it can easily overpower another color. Add some metallics or pearlescents to your colors to make the papers shimmer.

PREPARING THE PAPER

To properly prepare a sheet of paper, relax it in a tray or sink of water. Just drag the paper through the water, wetting both sides, and then let it drip for a moment before carrying it over to the Plexiglas and laying it flat. Bear down as you stroke the paper with a damp sponge to remove excess water, pressing out any air bubbles and flattening it completely. If any wrinkles remain in the paper, your patterning will highlight them and make them even more noticeable.

If you're working with small sheets of paper—less than 11 × 17 inches (27.9 × 43.2 cm)—you can sometimes just dampen them on either side with a sponge and then proceed without problems, but larger sheets will either dry out or buckle and make you wish you'd spent a little extra time wetting them.

Pressing out wrinkles and air bubbles prior to coating the dampened paper with paste.

APPLYING THE PASTE

Load a large 2- to 4-inch (5.1- to 10.2-cm) paint brush with paste and brush it evenly on your paper. Use horizontal strokes to cover the paper with a thin layer of paste, then go back over the paper with vertical strokes to assure a good color application. If you're using different colored pastes on the same sheet, brush in one direction only to avoid totally mixing the colors and making them muddy. Instead, try letting the colored pastes overlap slightly to make subtle color blends.

Patterning Principles

All-over repeat patterns are particularly effective in paste. A row of diagonal or horizontal lines crossed at regular intervals by vertical ones can be dramatic. A wavy line next to a straight one or a thin line placed next to a thick one can add contrast to a paste paper. Hard-edged designs drawn next to or over blurred impressions left by the bristles of a paint brush or a crumpled piece of plastic wrap also command interest. Overlapping patterns can create so much depth in a work that it looks almost three-dimensional. As you begin making designs, be sure to let yourself play a bit and really explore the medium; lots of pattern-making principles will reveal themselves to you. Remember to create some free-wheeling asymmetrical images from time to time to prevent yourself from becoming trapped in tight symmetrical ones.

Coating the dampened paper with paste, here colored with acrylics.

Making Combed Designs

Begin a combed design by applying your paste and then drawing a patterning tool through it. The tool will push the paste aside, creating a corridor that allows the paper color to show through. If the paste is too thin, or your paper was too wet, the paste will start to run back into the opening you created. In that case, let the paste sit on your sheet for a few minutes so that it can dry out a bit before you continue.

If all looks good, continue patterning, applying a firm but gentle pressure to avoid tearing the damp paper. Angling the combing tool toward you slightly helps make the movements smoother and the designs more pronounced. Vary the direction and type of movement you make to create straight lines, choppy zig-zags, or long gentle curves.

Making Prints in Paste

All-over printed paste designs can be made by stamping a coated paper with various objects. Rubber stamps and carved linoleum blocks can be used, as well as triangles, circles, or squares cut from balsa wood. Objects made of rubber, cork, metal, wood, and plastic will all displace the paste if you use them to strike the coated paper. To get the best image, wipe off the paste that clings to them before stamping a second time.

If your paste is slightly thick, carved wooden rolling pins and carved brayers will leave distinct impressions as you roll them over the paper. The intaglio cut, which forms a depression in the surface of the wood or rubber, will leave its image in the paste as the area around each cut pulls the paste away.

If materials are glued onto the roller, a raised or relief surface will be formed. In this case, the area surrounding the design will remain in the paste, as the raised image displaces the paste. Pieces of rubber or soft linoleum can be glued to a rolling pin to create a relief rolled image. Buttercut (see page 26), which cuts easily and has a self-adhesive backing, is ideal for making prints in paste.

Using rubber and metal graining combs to create a paste-paper design.

The designs featured in "haiku," a book by Annette Hollander, were created by stamping in paste. When extended, the book measures 6 × 30 inches (15.2 × 76.2 cm).

Using an intaglio-cut brayer to create a patterned paste paper. Brayer cut by Jeff Mathison.

Leaving Brush Impressions

Brushes of various widths and stiffness can be slapped against the pasted paper to leave soft feathered images. The brushes can be coated with the same or a different colored paste, or be used dry to create various effects. It's always gratifying to brush over an unsatisfactory sheet and begin slapping away, listening to the paste splat while you plan the next sheet. It's also gratifying to look down and find that relieving your aggressions has produced a stunning paste paper.

Making Dabbed Impressions

Sponges of different shapes and sizes with large or tiny holes can be dabbed against the pasted paper to leave soft mottled images. Use the sponges like the brushes, with or without paste or additional color, to obtain different images. Go over the sheet several times with different colors to create a multicolored sponged paper.

Crumple plastic wrap or wad up a piece of paper and dab it rapidly against the brushed sheet to make a beautiful soft blurred design, which can serve as a great background for additional combed movements.

Spattered Papers

Very thin colored paste can be brushed through a sieve to deliver a light spray of color, or spattered on with a toothbrush to create speckled designs. The paste can be spattered over a wet or dry pasted paper or on a new dry sheet.

Pulled Papers

Amazing landscape designs can be created by pressing pasted papers together and then pulling them apart. The suction created by these actions causes the paste to rise into a network of ridges that resembles trees, bushes, and mountains. Different effects can be achieved by using thick or thinner pastes, sandwiching string or lace between the pasted sheets or applying varying amounts of pressure to different parts of the sheet. You can work in one color or brush parts of one sheet with different colored pastes so that color blends will be created when the two sheets are sandwiched together. Narrow strips of cardboard or shaped cut-outs with or without paste can be placed on top of parts of a pasted sheet to create feathery veined patterns.

"Mile High Island," a paste-paper collage by Diane Maurer-Mathison, 10 × 15 inches (25.4 × 38.1 cm). The foliage pattern in the foreground of this work was created by pressing pasted papers together and then pulling them apart. The background was made by combing a paste design over a previously marbled sheet.

MULTIPLE-IMAGE PRINTS

If a dry, previously patterned sheet is dampened and coated with paste a second time, a multiple-image or ghost print can be made. Combed papers look especially sumptuous when they're coated with a gold or silver paste and patterned again. Acrylic interference colors can also make a paste paper shimmer if they're mixed with colored paste and just brushed on a sheet. Care must be taken if patterning with metal tools, however, as the redampened paste can be a bit fragile. Rubber and plastic implements are safer to use if you intend to make combed ghost prints.

DRYING THE PAPERS

Paste papers can be hung over racks or lines to dry. The ideal setup is to string lengths of 3-inch (7.6-cm) PVC plumbing pipe on a clothesline and drape wet papers over the pipe. The papers will dry with a slight curve in the center, but there won't be any troublesome crimps to press out.

PREPARING THE WORK SURFACE FOR ADDITIONAL SHEETS

When you've removed your first sheet to a drying area, use a wet sponge to completely remove any paste that's accumulated on your work surface before beginning another paper. I keep a bucket of water handy for this purpose. The water also enables me to squeeze out any paste from the sponge and proceed with sponging down the next dampened paper.

FLATTENING THE SHEETS

When your sheets are dry, you can flatten them by weighting them down with several books overnight or ironing them on their reverse sides.

A multiple-image paste design made with graining combs. The raspberry combed design was allowed to dry and the paper was redampened before being coated with gold paint and combed a second time.

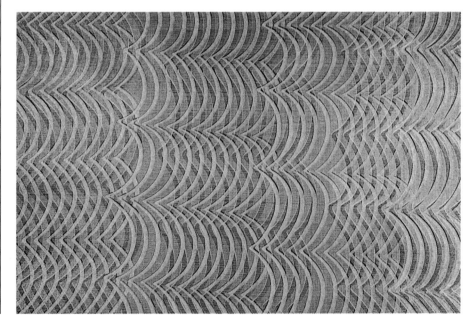

Batik

Batik or wax-resist designs are usually done on fabric. The technique is particularly well known in Indonesia, where it has been practiced for centuries. The interest in paper art has led some fiber artists to try their hand at paper batik, and the results are stunning, yielding luminescent batik papers and paper tapestries.

The principle behind the batik process is the same for fabric or paper: When wax is applied to a material it forms a resist that repels any liquid colors applied over it. If you splatter drops of wax on a sheet of white paper, for instance, and then coat the paper with a wash of blue watercolor, you'll wind up with a blue sheet of paper with white dots. If you then dip a brush in the wax, create a number of linear brush strokes on the blue paper, and then recoat the paper with green watercolor, you'll create a multicolor sheet. The paper will be green with white dots, still protected by the first waxing, and blue brushstrokes where the second waxing maintained the blue paint. The technique is actually much simpler than it sounds. To try your hand at it, you'll need:

- *Wax.* Paraffin, batik wax, and beeswax are all used for different effects. The paraffin tends to be more brittle. Usually a mix of beeswax and paraffin or batik wax is best to begin with.
- *A double boiler.* This is the safest way to melt the wax. A muffin pan set in an electric fry pan filled partially with water is another option.
- *Wax applicators.* Large and small disposable watercolor brushes, pipe cleaners, cardboard tubes, and batik tools that deliver a fine line of hot wax, such as tjanting needles, can all be used. Wax funnel pens that heat and dispense the wax at the same time are also available. These are a bit expensive, but worth the price if you intend to do a lot of fine-line batik.
- *A pencil.* You can draw designs before executing them in wax, if desired.
- *Paper.* Many types of paper, including watercolor paper, charcoal paper, and even typing paper, can be used for paper batik. Thin or absorbent papers would pose problems, however, as the wax could saturate the sheet and be hard to iron off.
- *Colors.* Rather transparent colors like liquid dyes and inexpensive watercolors can be used.
- *Color applicators.* Bamboo brushes, wide watercolor brushes, and poly foam brushes are all good tools for delivering a wash of color.
- *Newspapers.* You'll need lots of newspapers to absorb the wax as it's ironed out of a paper, and to protect tabletops from wax and color.
- *An iron.* An iron is needed to iron wax out of papers when you've finished decorating them. Use one without steam vents, if possible, as excess wax can clog the vents. Better yet, reserve an iron for paper batik only.

Detail of "Celebration Paper Batik," a beaded and stitched paper batik by Billi R. S. Rothove. 33 × 14¹/₂ inches (83.8 × 36.8 cm). Photo by Steve Ellis. (See page 1 for the complete work.)

Some of the materials for batik papers.

TRADITIONAL BATIK

Melt your batik wax or a mixture of paraffin and beeswax in a double boiler, being careful not to overheat it. The wax must be carefully monitored, as it can give off noxious smoke or catch on fire if it becomes too hot. Be sure to work with adequate ventilation. When the wax has melted, you can dip a brush or other wax applicator into it and begin making designs on a sheet of light-colored or white paper. The wax will begin to dry almost immediately, so you must work quickly. (This is one reason some artists prefer to plan out designs beforehand.)

When the first wax application is dry, apply a watercolor wash using a light-value color (such as yellow) that blends well with the color of your paper. Let the paint dry, then brush or splatter on more wax, followed by another wash of a darker harmonious color. Continue to build up layers of wax and color, bearing in mind that each coat of wax will maintain the last color applied.

When the final coat of color has dried, it's time to remove the wax from the sheet. Sandwich the paper batik between several layers of newspaper and press it with a warm iron, changing the newspaper until all the wax has been melted out of the sheet. The wax soaks into the newsprint laid over the sheet as you iron it, and can soak through the sheet onto the newspaper beneath it as well.

Brushing another layer of wax on a batik paper in progress. Several more layers of wax and color will be added to these sheets to finish them.

CREATING STRUCTURED DESIGNS

Although free-form brushed, splashed, and splattered batik papers are great fun to make, you can also be very methodical in your wax and color applications. When I asked Billi Rothove, a well-known fiber artist, if she would try some batik on paper instead of cloth, she graciously obliged and kept copious notes. (She also created a fabulous paper batik and may have been seduced away from fiber—at least for a while.) Billi's explanation of how she approached working with a new medium may be helpful to readers who desire a more structured way of creating designs:

The journey began with thumbnail sketches on graph paper of a variety of motifs and freehand designs, and placing them in various repetitive patterns to observe their relationships to each other. The graph paper provided a grid to help maintain similar sizes and intervals in the repeats while sketching. This quick and necessary process allowed time to consider the best selection of patterns and possible color combinations. It also helped define a direction to follow while experimenting with a new technique.

Some of the preliminary sheets that Billi created while experimenting with paper batik show an interesting combination of fine-line tools, controlled spattering, and brushwork. Others show how using cardboard tubes as wax stamping devices can create delightful repeat patterns.

Other stamping devices that can be dipped in wax and immediately stamped on the paper to leave a waxed impression include wooden dowels and cardboard box dividers. Pipe cleaners, too, can be twisted into flat designs, dipped in melted wax, and stamped on paper. If you leave a few inches of the pipe cleaner extending straight up, you'll have a convenient handle to work with.

Batik papers made with cardboard tubes and fine-line tools by Billi Rothove.

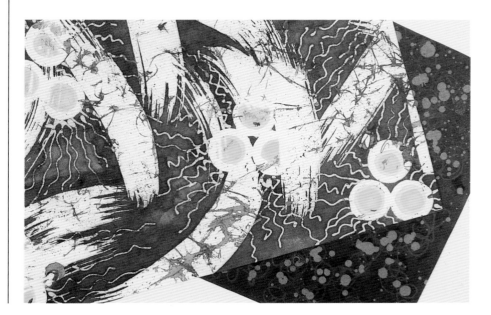

Orizomegami

The Japanese art of dyeing paper or fabric known as *orizomegami* can produce astonishing results. Some patterned papers resemble stained glass in their luminescence. Others have such a vivid symmetry that they look like images viewed through a kaleidoscope. A variety of dyeing techniques, such as *itajime* (board-clamp dyeing), *shibori* (a kind of tie-dye), and the more commonly practiced *fold and dye,* are all worth exploring.

Like batik, orizomegami patterning depends upon using resists to prevent dyes from reaching parts of the paper being decorated. Instead of using wax, however, resists are created by folding and pleating paper, then compressing the pleats by clipping them together with pieces of wood or plastic. String bindings and finger pressure on stacks of folded paper also help to keep bundles tight enough to form resists.

SIMPLE FOLD AND DYE

Dramatic results can be achieved by simply accordion-pleating absorbent paper and dipping the corners or sides of the folded bundle in dye. To begin this basic form of orizomegami, you'll need:

- *Paper.* Absorbent papers are perfect for simple fold-and-dye techniques. Block-printing papers, handmade papers, coffee filters, and various types of Japanese papers like mulberry and sumi-e can all be used. Harder Western papers can be tried, but they won't absorb colors as well. A bone folder may be necessary for heavier papers.
- *Colors.* Various types of inks and dyes can be used. Calligraphy inks, Japanese liquid pigment inks, fiber-reactive dyes, cold-water dyes like Rit, and professional egg dyes are also good to use. Food coloring gives great results but isn't permanent. Spraying acrylic medium on papers dyed with food coloring may help them to retain colors longer.
- *Color and water containers.* Wide-mouthed cups, muffin tins, or containers used to microwave eggs hold dyes as well as water for moistening papers before dyeing.
- *Hand towel and paper towels.* These are used to blot papers before and after dyeing.
- *Rubber gloves.* These are worn to protect hands from staining when handling dyes and dyed papers.
- *Newspapers and a plastic dropcloth.* Although the newspapers absorb most of the excess dye from your papers, sometimes the dye will bleed through them. It's a good idea to cover your work area with a plastic dropcloth just in case.

*Some of the materials
and equipment used
to make orizomegami
fold-and-dye papers.*

Simple fold-and-dye techniques can yield papers with soft, beautiful kaleidoscopic designs.

Folding the Paper

You can pleat your paper in a number of ways to prepare it for dyeing. The hill-and-valley accordion folds are the basis for many designs. Begin accordion pleating by folding the paper in half horizontally. Then fold each section in half again. Turn your paper and fold away from you each time, creating consistent, regular folds. You can also score your paper by indenting it slightly with a bone folder or other dull pointed tool before gathering it up into a series of accordion folds.

When you can no longer fold in one direction, take the pleated bundle of paper and fold it crosswise into a square or rectangle. Another option is to fold each pleated section into a triangle. Try these simple folding patterns and others shown below and opposite to prepare paper for dyeing.

Instead of neatly folding a sheet of paper, you can also twist it or bunch it into a ball to prepare it for dyeing. The patterned paper will have a mottled appearance, reflecting where some parts of the paper receive dye and other parts remain undyed. Brush or dip-dye the paper to color it, then overdye it to enhance designs (see "Dyeing the Folded Paper," page 88).

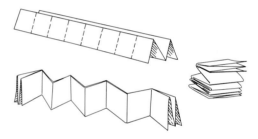

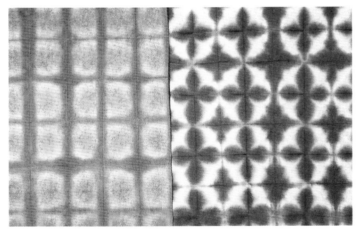

To make a square or rectangular folded bundle for dip- or brush-dyeing, accordion-pleat the paper by folding it back on itself in a series of square or rectangular folds.

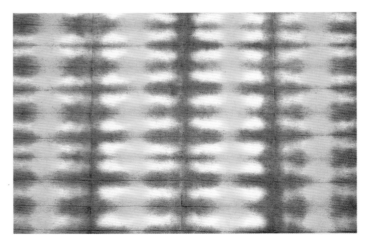

To make narrow rectangular folds, make 3/4-inch (1.9-cm) pleats in a sheet of paper, folding it back on itself in long sections.

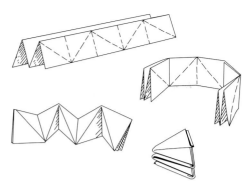

To make a triangular folded bundle, accordion-pleat the paper as described opposite, top, then fold it back on itself in a series of triangular accordion folds.

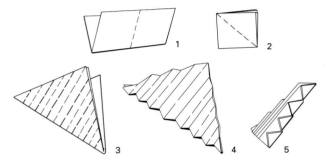

To create and pleat a triangular folded paper, (1) fold a square sheet of paper in half lengthwise, (2) fold it in half again, (3) bring the bottom left corner up to meet the top right corner to form a triangle, (4) then gather the triangle into narrow pleats. (5) The side view of the folded paper.

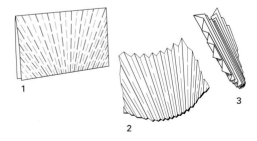

To create a series of radiating pleats in a sheet of paper, (1) fold the paper in half lengthwise, (2) then, starting from the center of the sheet, fold the paper to the left and then to the right to narrowly pleat it. (3) The side view of the folded paper. (Use clip clothespins to hold the paper for dipping or edge-dyeing.)

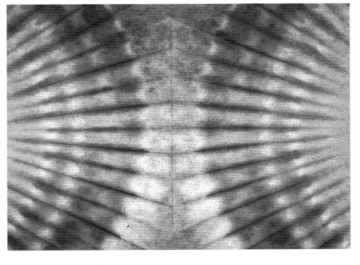

Prewetting the Folded Paper

Dip the folded bundle of paper in some water to moisten it, making it especially receptive to water-based dyes. Carefully press out most of the water with your fingers, then blot it with a hand towel until it's just damp. (To blot several bundles of moist paper at once, I place them side-by-side inside a towel and stand on it.) Premoistening the paper will give you softer, more diffused results. Try dip-dyeing some papers without wetting them first to achieve more hard-edged designs.

Dyeing the Folded Paper

Pour some of your color into a shallow container and dip a corner of the moist bundle of paper into the dye. The damp paper will wick the color deep into its folds. Compress the bundle between your thumb and forefinger to force the dye deeper into the center of the paper, or apply pressure and blot the bundle on a paper towel to stop the progression of the dye and force the extra color out of it.

Now dip another corner of the bundle into the same or another color and repeat the procedure. When all corners of your paper bundle have been dyed and blotted, place the bundle on newspaper or other scrap paper. If the dyed paper isn't too thin, you can open it out and see your masterpiece. If the paper is really fragile, however, it's best to wait until the bundle is almost dry before carefully unfolding it. Use caution: Wet paper tears easily!

Try dyeing the edges rather than the corners of another pleated bundle of paper to see how that influences patterning. You can also try experimenting with one of the following techniques:

Overdyeing. Refold a dry, already dyed paper in another configuration and dye it again. Even adding a few more spots of dye to a refolded sheet, or edge-dyeing a sheet that was previously corner-dyed, can prove rewarding.

Applying Dyes with Applicators. Design possibilities will increase if you add small bamboo brushes, squeeze bottles, and eyedroppers to your inventory of fold-and-dye equipment. Spot-dyeing with any of these tools, or applying color directly with brush markers, can add delightful accents to dyed papers. You can also use an applicator as the primary color delivery system for a pleated bundle of paper. It's sometimes easier to control color bleeds by applying color instead of dipping the paper into it.

Dipping a damp folded bundle of sumi-e paper into the dye.

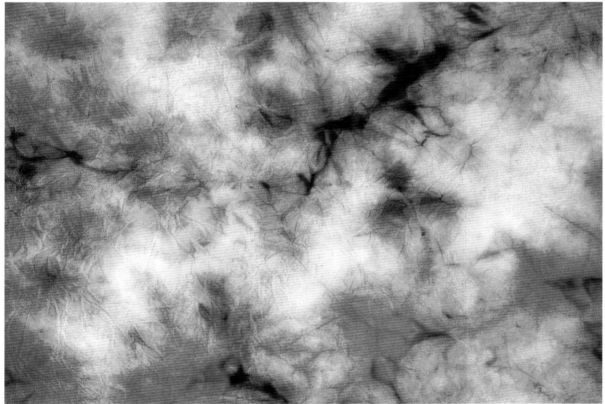

A design made by bunching a paper into a ball and then brush-dyeing it.

ITAJIME: "BOARD-CLAMP" AND CLIP DYEING

Sandwiching pleated papers between pieces of wood or plastic or clipping them between the jaws of clothespins or binder clips creates a tighter resist than simply folding and pleating, resulting in a more defined image. For this type of paper dyeing, you'll need several clamps or clips and color containers that are large enough to accommodate a bundle of paper with clamps attached. Absorbent medium-weight as well as lightweight papers are recommended for itajime.

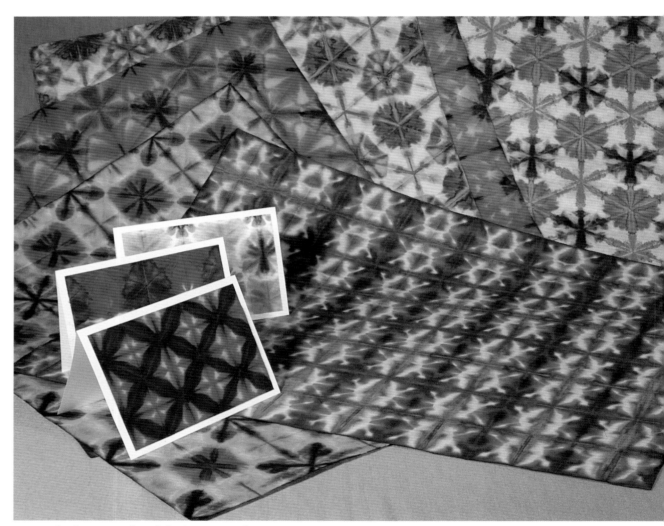

Itajime-dyed papers and cards by Susan Kristoferson.

Pleat a sheet of paper into a bundle, then sandwich it between two pieces of nonabsorbent material, such as wood molding, chopsticks, tongue depressors, or triangular, square, or rectangular pieces of wood or Plexiglas. Then use rubber bands, binder clips, or plastic spring-clip clothespins to clamp the materials in place. Plastic clothespins (which can be rinsed clean) and binder clips can also be used by themselves to bind a thin pleated bundle in various places. When the resist materials are in place, dip or apply color to the bundle as described on page 88.

Heavier, nonabsorbent papers can also be clamped and dyed if you submerge them in the dye bath. The length of time it takes to dye a paper bundle successfully will depend upon its size and the absorbency of the papers used. Most small bundles of medium-weight papers will need to be immersed in dye for about an hour. Heavier papers may need 4 to 24 hours to soak up enough color to produce a good design.

The tightness of the binding will also influence design. Very tight bindings will permit only the outside layers of the bundle to be colored. Refolding a sheet of paper for overdyeing so that the innermost, undyed layers are on the outside is often quite effective. NOTE: When binding papers with rubber bands, leave them in place until the paper is almost dry to avoid tearing it during their removal.

A number of folded bundles prepared for clamp-dyeing.

SHIBORI OR TIE-DYE

Binding papers with string offers even more design possibilities. If papers are bound tightly, the string forms a resist, preserving the color of the paper underneath. If string is used to bind a sheet of paper to a pole or other cylindrical base, and the paper is then scrunched by grasping it at either end and pushing it toward the center of the pole, the string will not only form a resist but will play an important part in forcing the paper into tiny pleats. The action is much like that used to scrunch and pleat a soda straw wrapper.

The cylindrical base can be a broom handle, soda bottle, or PVC pipe, and the wrapping can be done clockwise or counterclockwise and at different angles to achieve different effects. Papers of various weights can be wrapped with string, waxed linen thread, or dental floss. The wrapped poles can be submerged in dyes, or, for more absorbent papers, dye can be poured over them as they rest over dye containers.

Terri Fletcher uses shibori and other resist techniques on cotton rag tracing vellum to create scrunched, dyed, and stitched artworks. Before binding her papers, Terri draws on them with colored pencils or crayons (which also act as a resist against the dye). She also collages cellophane-tape resists on one side of the paper only, which allows some of the dye to seep into the paper for a gentle coloration. Terri cuts the paper into strips 3 to 6 inches (7.6 to 15.2 cm) wide before dyeing them with Procion fabric dyes.

After the dyed strips are dry, flattened, and embellished once more with crayon and colored pencil, Terri begins wrapping them around plastic plumbing pipe, binding them with dental floss, and scrunching them. The scrunching prevents the dye from reaching the innermost folds of the paper, which adds more interest to its pleated texture. The wrapped pipes are then soaked in a second dye bath for 2 to 4 hours. While the shibori-dyed strips are still wet, Terri unwinds them so they can be stitched, taking care not to remove the pleats. When they are thoroughly dry, she assembles the strips on a sewing machine, using different types of stitches to enhance the image. (For another example of Terri's work, see "Stitched Collage," page 124.)

FLATTENING ORIZOMEGAMI PAPERS

Although the textured appearance of many folded or pleated and dyed papers is an integral part of their design, you can flatten them if desired by simply pressing them with a cool iron.

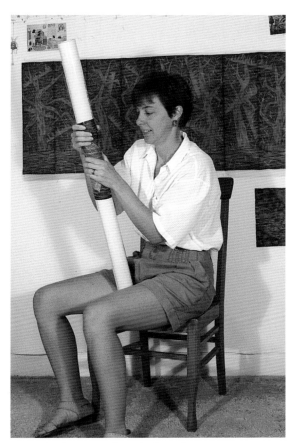

The bound and pleated papers soaking in the dye bath.

Terri Fletcher scrunching the bound paper to create tiny pleats.

Pulling the shibori-dyed papers back into strips before drying and finally stitching them together.

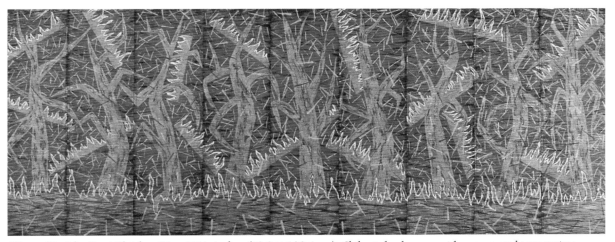

"Forest Fire" by Terri Fletcher, 21 × 54¹/₂ inches (53.3 × 138.4 cm). Shibori-dyed paper with crayon and tape resists.

Suminagashi Marbling

Suminagashi, the oldest form of marbling, began in Japan or possibly China over 800 years ago. The gentle, almost meditative, suminagashi techniques involve floating colors on the surface of water, gently blowing or fanning the colors into a design, then applying an absorbent paper to make a contact print. The flowing suminagashi designs can be made in the traditional Japanese colors of black and blue, in subtle pastel hues, or in bold colors for a more graphic look. Single-image papers can be enjoyed for their jagged or meandering lines of color, or papers can be marbled a second time to produce complex patterns of intersecting lines and colors. To explore suminagashi marbling, you'll need the following materials and equipment:

- *Marbling tray.* Basically any kind of tray about 2 inches (5.1 cm) deep—for example, a photo tray, kitty litter pan, or purchased marbling tray—will work for suminagashi marbling. You can also try using a baking pan, but keep in mind that many baking pans are coated with materials that can make colors sink. (This problem can usually be rectified by slipping the pan inside a plastic garbage bag before filling it with water.)

    You can also build a proper 13^1/$_2$- × 23-inch (34.9- × 55.9-cm) marbling tray with a spiffy rinsing and draining area using lightweight ^{1}/$_4$-inch (6-mm) plywood. Start by cutting the plywood in pieces as follows:

    Two 13^1/$_2$- × 23-inch (34.9 × 55.9-cm) pieces, one for the base and one for the cover/rinseboard (cut with a "V" and notched as shown opposite)

    Two 1^3/$_4$- × 23-inch (4.5- × 55.9-cm) pieces, for the long sides of the tray

    Three 1^3/$_4$- × 13-inch (4.5- × 33-cm) pieces, two for the short sides and one for the drain partition (with one long edge cut at a 45-degree angle)

    One 2- × 12^3/$_4$-inch (5.1- × 32.4-cm) piece, for a skimboard. (Optional, but useful in oil marbling; see page 105.)

    Two ^{1}/$_4$- × ^{1}/$_4$- × 18^3/$_4$-inch (6-mm × 6-mm × 47.6-cm) edge strips for the rinseboard

    Drill a ^{3}/$_4$-inch (6-mm) hole in one corner of the base. Sand all the pieces smooth. Glue and clamp the tray edges together, then glue the rinseboard strips in place. (If modifying these instructions to build a larger tray, reinforce the tray corners and edges of the drain partition with brass screws.) Paint the bottom of the tray white and waterproof the entire tray with two coats of Zip Guard Urethane; unlike some urethanes, this particular brand will not cause paint sinkage.

- *Water.* You'll need enough to fill the marbling tray to a depth of 1^1/$_2$ inches (3.8 cm).

The components and dimensions of a proper marbling tray.

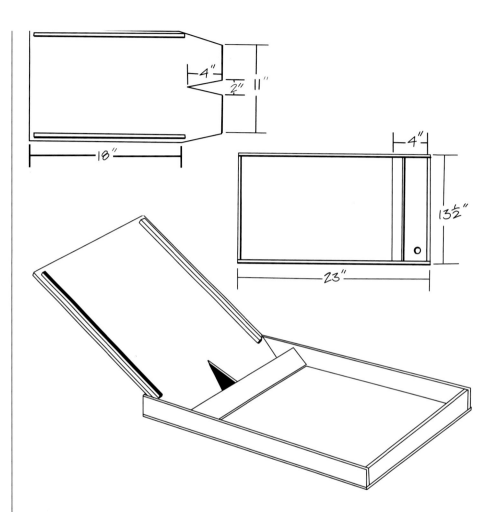

Some of the materials and equipment used for suminagashi marbling. Although not essential, a fan can help create patterns with traditional jagged lines.

- *Colors.* Cake and liquid sumi inks like Boku Undo colors work well. Many drawing inks, such as Pelikan and Speedball, can also be used. The pigmented varieties impart the richest color.
- *Photo-Flo 200.* Manufactured by Kodak, this photographic surfactant (a substance that decreases the surface tension of water) is added to some brands of ink or paint (such as Boku Undo inks) to help them float and spread on the surface of the water. In addition, a dispersant solution used to control the color once it's been applied to the water can be made by mixing one drop of Photo-Flo with 1 teaspoon (5 ml) of water. This solution acts as a kind of "invisible color" that pushes each circle of color it touches into a large narrow ring, and can also be used to preserve open areas in designs.
- *Watercolor mixing tray.* A shallow watercolor mixing tray that holds about 1 teaspoon (5 ml) of color is ideal for suminagashi marbling. An ice cube tray can be used as a substitute color container.
- *Eyedroppers.* These are used to transfer color from original containers into the mixing tray.
- *Brushes.* Inexpensive bamboo watercolor brushes about 1 inch (2.5 cm) long and tapered to a point are needed to apply the inks to the water. Either the #2 or #4 sizes are perfect. You'll need at least four of them.
- *Brush rest.* This is optional, but very helpful. An inexpensive plastic type works fine.
- *Paper.* Absorbent papers are best for suminagashi marbling. Japanese papers such as kozo, Moriki, and Okawara, as well as Speedball block-printing paper, all marble well. Handmade papers and coffee filters also work. Some typing papers with a high cotton content will also pick up an image, although it may be pale. Experiment with various papers.
- *Newspapers.* Newspapers help protect tabletops, and, when cut into 2-inch (5.1-cm) strips, can be used to skim off excess color that remains after a print is made.
- *Hand protection.* Thin latex surgical gloves or barrier hand cream can be used to protect your hands from staining.
- *Rinsing equipment.* A drain bucket and water jug are needed to rinse some papers.
- *Rinsing support.* If you use a makeshift tray without a rinsing area and your papers have an excess of color that needs to be rinsed off, you'll need some sort of support to carry the wet sheet to a sink or nearby hose. Either a cookie sheet or piece of Plexiglas can be used.
- *Drying equipment.* Although drying racks designed for clothes can be used to hold wet papers, the ideal setup for drying marbled sheets is lengths of PVC pipe strung over a clothesline.

*"Eight Sumi Squares"
by Jennifer Philippoff,
a multiple-image
suminagashi marbling
with vinyl cut-out accents
measuring 10 × 18
inches (25.4 × 45.7 cm).*

SKIMMING

Before you begin marbling, you'll need to skim off any dust that has settled on the water in your tray. You'll also need to skim to remove any excess color that remains on your tray between prints. Skimming is especially important when using drawing inks, as their residue will often prevent other colors from floating. To skim, just drag a 2-inch (5.1-cm) strip of newspaper across the water's surface. If conditions get really dirty, you can, of course, just refill your tray with clean water.

TESTING THE COLOR

To determine whether the color you're using needs a drop of Photo-Flo to make it disperse properly, transfer 1 teaspoon (5 ml) of color into your mixing tray, dip your brush into it, wipe off any excess, then touch the tip of the brush to the surface of the water. The color should rapidly spread into a circle about 3 inches (7.6 cm) in diameter. If the color doesn't spread, or if it sinks, stir a single drop of Photo-Flo into the color in the mixing tray, then test it again. If it's going to work for suminagashi marbling, it should now float fine.

It's important to make sure that any color to which Photo-Flo has been added be stirred well and often. If it isn't, the Photo-Flo will settle out and the colors will begin to sink, tempting you to add even more Photo-Flo, which, paradoxically, will make your colors sink. (If too much surfactant gets mixed into the water in your tray, it will alter the water's surface tension so much that colors can't push against it to float.)

To skim off excess color, hold the newspaper strip as shown and pull it down the length of the tray, depositing color residue in the drain area.

APPLYING AND PATTERNING THE COLORS

Fill three sections of your mixing tray: two with different colored inks and another with the dispersant solution of Photo-Flo and water. Start by holding two brushes, one loaded with well-stirred and tested color and the other loaded only with the dispersant. Barely touch the center of the water-filled tray with the color-loaded brush to release a drop of color. Now touch the center of the expanded drop of color with the tip of the dispersant brush. The dispersant solution will propel the circle of color into a large ring.

Alternately apply colors and dispersant until a number of concentric clear and colored rings are formed, then gently blow them into a design. If you blow from the side of the tray, the lines of color will be more meandering. A hearty burst of air from overhead will produce a pattern with more jagged lines. You can also fan the colors with a piece of cardboard or a Japanese fan.

Alternately apply color and dispersant to build up a number of concentric rings.

Fanning the floating rings of color into a jagged design. A hearty burst of air from overhead will also produce jagged rings of color.

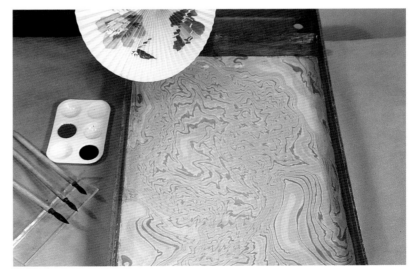

Although exuberant stirring usually sinks floating colors, you can create subtle combed designs by dragging a single hair through them. I created a special tool that makes interesting patterns by taping a single cat whisker to the end of dowel. (I don't recommend trimming your pet's whiskers—just be on the lookout for any stray "gifts" that are left lying around.)

Japanese suminagashi masters traditionally applied inks to water holding two brushes loaded with color in one hand and a brush charged with dispersant (a pine oil) in the other. They usually worked in black and indigo only, depositing between fifty and a hundred rings before patterning them. Once you've become comfortable with applying color and dispersant with two brushes, try working with three, just as the Japanese masters did.

Work in as many colors as you choose, creating concentric rings by alternating color with dispersant or applying one color on top of another without using dispersant. Work in the center of the tray or deposit color in various sections, building up as many rings of color as you choose before depositing color in a new location.

You won't have much color sinkage if you remember to apply your colors gently. And if you apply your colors with just the tip of the brush (taking care not to dunk it), you won't run the risk of diluting your colors by reloading a water-soaked brush.

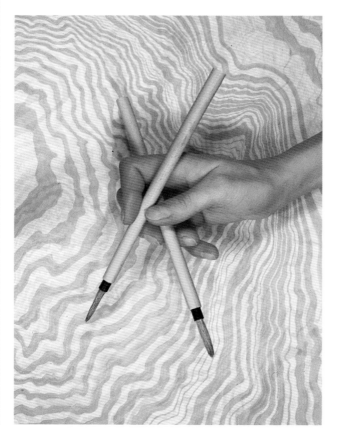

You can deposit color more quickly by holding two color-charged brushes in one hand and the dispersant brush in the other.

MAKING THE PRINT

When the colors are patterned, carefully lay a sheet of absorbent paper on top of them to make a contact print. Try not to shift the paper or flop it down or you'll disturb the design you've created and possibly trap air beneath the paper, creating an unsightly void in the pattern.

One way to apply the paper is to hold it by diagonal corners so that it droops in the center. Steady one hand on the far corner of the tray, then, while still holding the paper, ease one edge onto the color. In one fluid motion, lower the rest of the sheet onto the floating color. If you're marbling very thin sheets of paper, leave the near edge of the sheet dry so you can pick the paper up without tearing it. After the sheet has made contact with the color, lift it off and carry it to the drying area or, if necessary, place it on a rinseboard and rinse off excess color.

Once you've finished your marbling session, be sure to clean trays and brushes with water only, as any soap residue (a surfactant) will cause problems during your next session.

Make the suminagashi print by steadying one hand on the far corner of the tray and easing the far edge of the paper onto the color. Hold that edge steady while you lower the rest of the sheet. Don't let go of either edge until the entire paper is down.

Rinsing excess color from the marbled paper. A tray with a rinsing area makes this process easy.

OVERMARBLING

When a marbled sheet is dry, it can be marbled a second time to produce an overmarbled or "ghost" print like the one shown below, left. The intersecting lines create new patterns and colors and often save a previously uninteresting print.

Unfortunately, marbled prints made with some drawing inks repel a second coat of color and can't be overmarbled. Also, certain brands of inks (such as Higgins) behave erratically and dry so quickly that they tend to break up on the surface of the water. Sometimes these characteristics can be used to create novel effects similar to those shown in "Ice Breaker" (below, right).

FLATTENING MARBLED PAPERS

If you place dry marbled sheets under books or a board, they'll dry quite flat. Sheets may also be ironed on a low setting.

A double suminagashi print with intersecting lines and colors by Diane Maurer-Mathison. By varying the amount of time the brush remains in contact with the water, you can deposit more or less ink and create thick or thin lines of color.

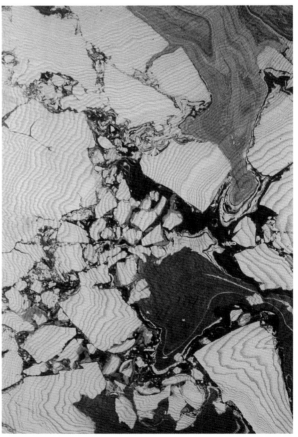

"Ice Breaker," a double suminagashi print by Milena Hughes, 26 × 18 inches (66 × 45.7 cm).

Oil Marbling

Oil marbling is easily recognized by its rich flowing swirls and spots of color. Dappled areas with little beads of reticulated paint are also a delightful feature of this type of marbling. Oil marbling has been admired and practiced for centuries and was used extensively by 18th-century European artisans to create endpapers and cover papers for their handmade books.

Although oil marbling is similar to suminagashi marbling (see pages 94–102) in that colors are floated on a liquid, the colors are patterned, and a sheet of paper is applied to the colors to make a contact print, the materials and techniques used are quite different. In addition to being floated on water, oil marbling colors can be floated on a thickened liquid known as *marbling size* and patterned to produce a crude combed design.

Unfortunately, oil marbling is a good deal more messy and odorous than suminagashi marbling. You'll want to have good ventilation and an exhaust fan in your marbling studio, even if you're using the newer nontoxic solvents. Devotees of oil marbling all claim that the extra steps necessary to work with oil paints are well worth the effort. When you see the vibrant papers you can achieve with this medium, you'll probably agree. The equipment and materials needed for oil marbling include:

- *Marbling tray.* See page 94 for more information. You can use a purchased, constructed, or makeshift tray for oil marbling, but the tray must be reserved for oil marbling alone. Any residue of paints or thinner on the tray or marbling tools will make suminagashi colors sink.

A multiple-image oil-marbled paper by Paul Maurer.

- *Water.* Fill the marbling tray with water to a depth of 1½ inches (3.8 cm).
- *Colors.* Any oil-based paints or inks, either liquid or paste (both tube colors or nonliquid colors such as etching inks in cans), can be used. Artist's oils, lithography inks, etching inks, and printer's inks usually produce good results. Gold and silver decorator's enamels and some sign-painting paints also work for oil marbling.
- *Photo-Flo 200.* A drop or two of Photo-Flo can often help problem colors spread on water or size.
- *Linseed oil.* Linseed oil makes oil colors more luminous and helps soften paste colors.
- *Mineral spirits or Safe Solve.* These thinners dilute oil-based paints, help disperse color, and clean oil marbling equipment. Safe Solve is a nontoxic turpentine substitute and safer to use than other paint thinners.
- *Color containers.* Use metal or glass containers; thinners for oil-based media will deteriorate some plastics.
- *Color stirring sticks.* Dowels or Popsicle sticks can be used to stir the color and mix additives into it.

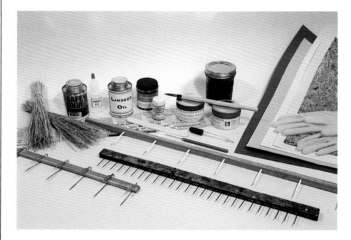

Some of the materials and equipment used for oil marbling.

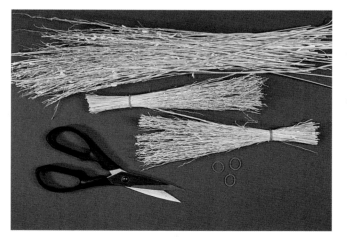

Broomstraw whisks are easy to make. Just bind the straw with a rubber band. You'll need a whisk for each color used.

- *Color applicators.* Eyedroppers and small bamboo brushes, like those used for suminagashi marbling (see page 96), can be used to deposit color on the water or size. Another important tool is the straw broom whisk. To make a whisk, purchase a natural straw broom or loose broomcorn and cut 6-inch (15.2-cm) lengths of straw from it. (The grassy or stiff ends of the straw can be used.) Compress the straw into a 1-inch-wide (2.5-cm-wide) bundle and wrap a rubber band around it. Make several whisks— you'll need one for each color used.
- *Paper.* Special papers aren't necessary for oil marbling. As long as a paper can withstand getting wet and its surface isn't so slick that it would repel color, it can be oil-marbled.
- *Newspapers.* Newspapers are used for making skim strips and for covering work areas.
- *Skimboard.* For removing bubbles introduced by blending when marbling on a size. See page 94 for instructions on how to make one.
- *Paper towels.* Use these for blotting excess paint off newly marbled sheets and for cleanups.
- *Drying equipment.* See page 96 for advice on creating a drying station for marbled papers.
- *Cleanup equipment.* A scrub brush, dish detergent, and nonchlorine powdered cleanser will be needed for cleaning up. Pipe cleaners are also needed for cleaning eyedroppers.
- *Mask.* It's a good idea to wear a respirator when working with oil paints and thinners. An exhaust fan can help eliminate harmful fumes.
- *Rubber gloves or oil-repellant barrier hand cream.* Use one of these to protect your hands from staining and the harsh effects of thinners.

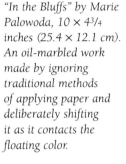

"In the Bluffs" by Marie Palowoda, 10 × 4³/₄ inches (25.4 × 12.1 cm). An oil-marbled work made by ignoring traditional methods of applying paper and deliberately shifting it as it contacts the floating color.

MIXING THE COLOR

If you're marbling with liquid oils, pour about 1 inch (5.1 cm) of well-stirred color into a container. Then add about one-fifth as much linseed oil and enough thinner to bring the color to a milky consistency.

If you're working with paste oils, start by putting about 2 tablespoons (30 ml) of color in a container, then add one-fourth as much linseed oil. Use a dowel or stick to push and stir the oil into the paste until it is smooth. Add a bit more linseed oil to bring the color to a creamy consistency. (If the color remains stringy, you may have to homogenize it with a mortar and pestle.) When the color is well creamed, stir in enough thinner to bring it to a milky consistency.

TESTING THE COLOR

To test a color, first skim the water-filled marbling tray with a strip of newspaper to remove surface skin and dust. Then insert a whisk into a well-mixed color, stir, then tap off any excess paint. Hold the whisk above the tray and tap it against a stick or your finger to broadcast droplets of paint. The paint should float and spread while retaining its color.

If the paint spreads so much that it becomes transparent, add more color to your mixture. If it sinks to the bottom of the tray, it's probably too thick and requires additional thinner. Test all the colors to make sure they respond correctly.

Usually, if all the colors test out individually, they'll work together in the marbling tray. Sometimes, however, a particular color alters the surface tension of the water so much that when another color follows it, it can't spread enough to float. To solve this dilemma, either apply the colors in a sequence that keeps them all afloat, or add Photo-Flo or more thinner to the hesitant color to make it spread more.

Testing the thinned color by applying it with a whisk. The color should float and spread without becoming transparent.

MARBLING ON WATER

Use whisks, brushes, or eyedroppers to apply the oil colors to the size, remembering to stir well. If you're using an eyedropper, fill it with color and keep pressure on the bulb so you don't draw in air and wind up depositing bubbles of color on the water. Skim the size, then apply as many colors as you like in various sections of the marbling tray. The colors will wander in and around each other to form designs. It's a bit frustrating to spot a terrific image, then watch it disappear before you can lay down a sheet of paper to print it, but that's the nature of marbling on water—especially with oil colors that seem to have their own agenda.

Make a print by lowering a sheet of paper onto the floating colors. Use the same technique discussed in suminagashi marbling (see page 101), working slowly and carefully to avoid trapping air bubbles beneath the sheet. When your sheet has been printed, lift it out of the marbling tray and place it on your drainboard, or on some newspaper if you're using a makeshift tray. Use a paper towel to blot off excess color before carrying the sheet to your drying rack or lines. Skim off excess color from the water before beginning another print.

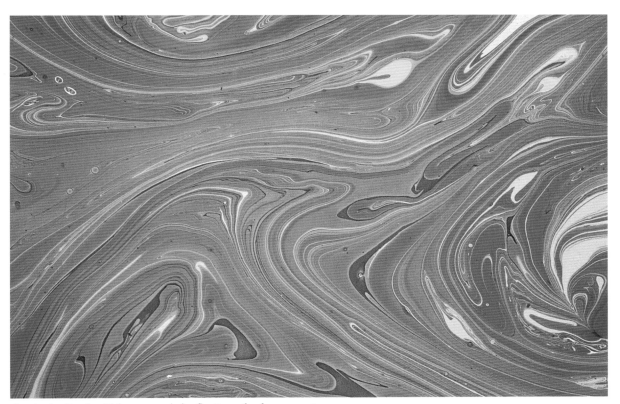

A print by Sandra Holzman made by floating oil colors on water.

MARBLING ON A SIZE

A thickened marbling size, which is made by mixing water with either methyl cellulose or powdered *carrageenan* (an extract of Irish seaweed available from a marbling supply house), will allow you to gain some control over the floating colors. (Other size possibilities to explore for novel effects are cornstarch and liquid starch.) Because oil colors on a size are unable to move as freely as they do on water, you can pattern the colors to a limited degree.

In addition to the materials and equipment noted previously, you'll also need a tablespoon for measuring out the powdered size, a large pot for mixing the size, a water jug for dispensing the rinse water, and a rinseboard and bucket or nearby sink to allow you to rinse excess size from your marbled sheets.

Making a Methyl Cellulose Size

Follow the directions provided with the methyl cellulose you purchased, stirring well and adding enough water to bring the size to the consistency of milk. (The recipe we use is 4 tablespoons [60 g] of methyl cellulose to about 6 pints [2.8 l] of water.) Let the mixture stand for about 15 minutes until it becomes clear and smooth. Then pour it into your tray, skim off the bubbles, and apply your paints.

Making a Carrageenan Blender Size

Because carrageenan is a food additive, you can use your kitchen blender to mix up the size. The basic recipe calls for mixing 2 flat tablespoons (30 g) of powdered carrageenan with 1 gallon (3.8 l) of water. Begin by measuring out the amounts of carrageenan and water you'll need for your tray. (A 13½- × 23-inch [34.3- × 58.4-cm] tray will use about a gallon of size.) Fill your blender about two-thirds full of water and turn it on low. When the water is moving, slowly tap in 1 scant tablespoon (15 g) of carrageenan and blend for several seconds to dissolve it. Then add enough water to bring the blender to three-quarters full and blend another minute before pouring the mixture into a waiting pot or bucket.

Repeat until you've mixed all the size with the water. Stir the mixture, then pour it into your tray to fill it to a level of about 1½ inches (3.8 cm). If you let the size stand overnight, the bubbles introduced by blending will dissipate. If you want to begin marbling immediately, you'll need to spend time removing the bubbles with a skimboard before applying your colors.

When making carrageenan blender size, turn the blender on "low," then tap the carrageenan powder into the moving water a little at a time.

Using a skimboard to remove bubbles introduced by blending the size.

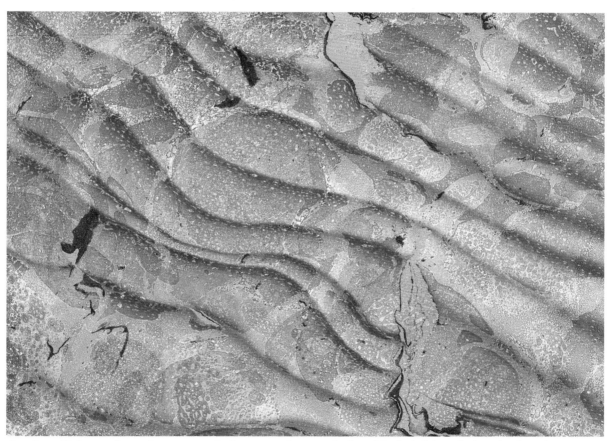

An oil-marbled paper by Paul Maurer. Paul often moves the paper back and forth slightly as he lays the sheet down to create rippled bands of color.

Colors floating on a marbling size can be patterned with a stylus, toothpick, hair pick, or piece of broom straw. Combs and rakes can also be made for manipulating colors. Push brass or stainless dressmaker pins through a length of balsawood or glue pins between strips of wood to make a comb. To make a simple rake, slip drapery hooks over a piece of molding at about 2-inch (5.1-cm) intervals. Another more substantial type of rake that breaks up the color into a finer pattern can be made by drilling holes in a piece of wood molding and gluing in sharpened dowels or slipping in plastic teeth used for hair curlers. When making either type of rake, be sure to set the teeth far enough apart to allow you to rake in a horizontal as well as a vertical direction.

To marble, skim the size and apply your colors with whisks, brushes, or eyedroppers. Print the image without patterning, pattern the colors at random, or follow the diagrams on pages 112–113 to create traditional designs. The combed patterns will have feathered, rather indistinct edges. Sometimes—especially if you're using Safe Solve as a thinner—they'll also be stippled, with tiny beads of color adding to their unusual appearance.

Because oil colors also like to pattern themselves, we sometimes create designs by applying the paints with a whisk and then walking away from the tray, returning after about an hour to see what's happened in our absence. Sometimes the paints break up into beautiful designs that resemble lichen. A wide range of images are possible with oil marbling.

RINSING AND DRYING

After applying paper to the size and making a print, place your marbled sheet on a rinseboard and rinse it with water to remove any excess size that may be clinging to it. Blot off excess color with a paper towel, then carry the sheet to a drying area. Once the sheet is dry (which can take several days under humid conditions), it can be ironed flat or marbled a second time to create a more complex, multiple-image pattern.

CLEANUP

Clean tools and equipment with thinner, carefully removing all residue of color. Then scrub the equipment with a brush and a mild powdered cleanser to remove the thinner film before rinsing thoroughly. Use thinner to clean the brushes and whisks, rinse them in warm water, then work dish detergent into them to remove the thinner film. Clean eyedroppers with thinner and then soap, using a pipe cleaner to reach all parts of the dropper and cap. Rinse all equipment thoroughly.

Some rakes, a comb, and a stylus used to pattern oil-marbled papers. The paper shown was patterned by drawing spirals in the floating color with a stylus.

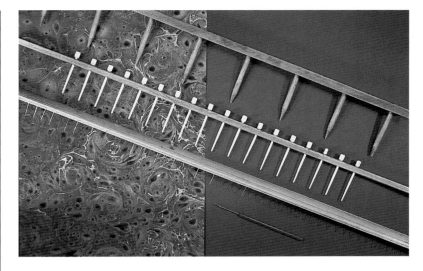

Using a 2-inch (5.1-cm) rake to pattern oil color on a carrageenan size.

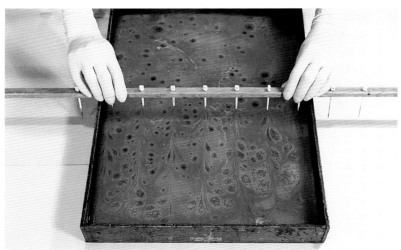

Using a comb with teeth spaced ¹/₂ inch (1.3 cm) to pattern oil colors.

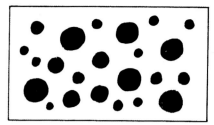

To recreate these oil-marbled patterns made on a carrageenan size by Paul Maurer, follow the diagrams and move your rake or comb in the direction of the arrows. Dotted lines indicate previous comb or rake movements.

1. Apply color with a whisk to make a stone pattern.

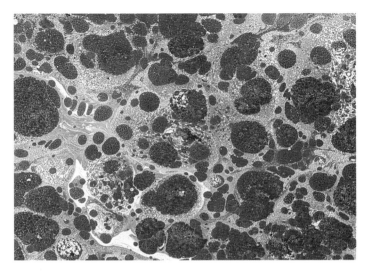

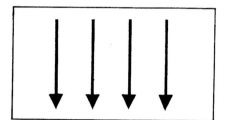

2. Apply color as in step 1, then pull a marbling rake toward you to create the first stage of the get-gel pattern.

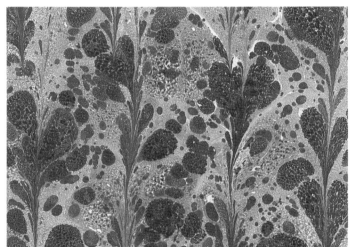

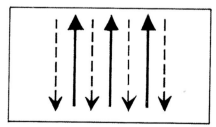

3. After completing step 2, push the rake away from you, bisecting the previous pass to complete the second stage of the get-gel pattern.

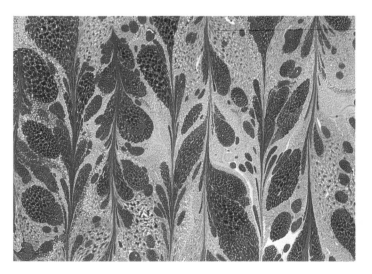

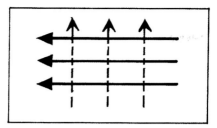

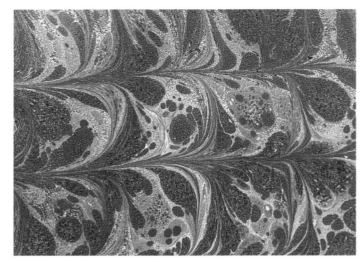

4. *Rake right to left across the results of step 3 to create this design, the third stage of the get-gel pattern.*

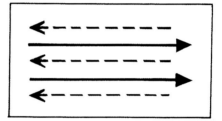

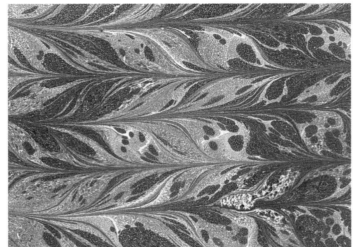

5. *To finish the get-gel pattern, rake left to right, bisecting step 4.*

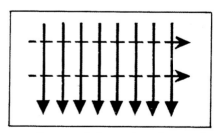

6. *Pull a ¹/₂-inch (1.3-cm) comb toward you over step 5 to create a loose Nonpareil design.*

PAPERCRAFT TECHNIQUES

By now you've probably produced lots of gorgeous handmade and hand-decorated papers. Some, no doubt, are in a stack to be matted and framed as art prints. Others may have been made into cards or used in bookbinding projects. Some may be squirreled away for use in specific artworks and others (the ugly ones) may be on their way to the kitchen blender to be resurrected as handmade paper.

If you've overmarbled, overprinted, and overdyed, and still can't save the papers that didn't quite work out, this chapter of *Paper Art* offers hope. Homely papers can be redeemed by cutting them, folding them, weaving them, or using them in collages. The papercraft techniques in this section will show you lots of ways to use the papers you've produced, purchased, or scavenged to best advantage.

Detail of "Are We?" by Arlene Gitomer, 20 × 21 inches (50.8 × 53.3 cm). This stitched collage combines handmade paper, embroidery, and painting with printed acetate.

Working with Paper

By learning a few simple techniques and investing in some inexpensive equipment, you'll make paper a cooperative partner in your paper art instead of an adversary that must be tamed.

BASIC PAPERCRAFT EQUIPMENT

- *Scoring tool.* Use an awl, a bone folder, or the end of a ball-tipped burnisher for this purpose.
- *Cutting tools.* These include a cutting mat or piece of glass with taped edges, plus a mat knife, scissors, and an X-Acto knife.
- *Metal ruler.* Use the edge of a metal ruler to guide your scoring and cutting tools.
- *Burnishing tool.* A bone folder or plastic burnishing tool can be used to sharpen folds and bond glued papers.
- *Large and small glue brushes.* These are used for collage, pop-ups, and paper sculpture. My favorites are #12 and #6 Gainsborough brushes by Grumbacher.

BASIC TECHNIQUES

Finding a Paper's Grain. All machine-made papers have what's known as a *grain,* which is the direction in which the paper fibers line up. (Handmade papers have no grain, as their fibers are distributed randomly.) It's important that a paper's grain be determined and followed when scoring, folding, or bonding (gluing) papers. Otherwise, your constructions may be distorted and warped and your fold lines may wind up irregular and cracked. Tearing and cutting will also be much easier if you do so in a direction parallel to the grain of the paper.

To test for grain in a sheet of paper, bend it in half. If it collapses easily, you're bending with the grain. If it resists, you're bending cross-grain. Mat board and illustration board will also communicate grain direction when you attempt to bend them.

If a paper collapses easily when you attempt to bend it, you're bending with the grain. If it offers resistance, you're bending cross-grain.

Scoring. Scoring—using an awl, bone folder, the end of a ball-tipped burnisher, or another tool to crease a paper's surface—prepares paper for folding. To score a sheet, hold a metal ruler against the desired fold line and, using the ruler as a guide, drag the point of the tool down the length of the ruler. When scoring light- to medium-weight papers, you'll want to indent—not break—the surface, and bend *away* from, not into, the fold line. When scoring very heavy papers or mat board, cut into the top layer of paper with a mat knife.

Cutting. Always have a sharp blade in your mat knife or X-Acto knife. Hold the knife upright and slide it against the edge of a metal ruler to cut paper or board. Cut on a cutting mat or against glass, as cutting into cardboard dulls a knife blade quickly. If you're trying to cut mat board or other heavy material, don't attempt to do so in one pass; make several cuts instead.

Burnishing. Burnishing paper with a bone folder sharpens folds and bonds glued papers by pushing out wrinkles and air bubbles. To avoid damaging or adding a shine to papers being burnished, cover them with a sheet of tracing or waxed paper. When bonding one glued paper to another, hold the burnishing tool on its side and work from the center of the sheet outward to flatten it.

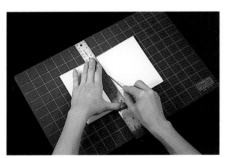

Scoring a sheet of paper with an awl. A light touch will indent the sheet, while exerting pressure will break its surface.

To use an X-Acto knife to slice into a sheet of paper, hold the knife upright and slide it against the edge of a metal ruler.

Using a bone folder to sharpen a crease on a reverse-pleated triangle.

By placing tracing or waxed paper over bonded papers before burnishing, you can protect your decorated sheets.

Collage

Gluing materials to a surface to create a design is often thought of as a 20th-century invention. But paper collage has been practiced for centuries. As early as the 12th century, Japanese calligraphers copied poems on collaged sheets of cut and shaped papers. The art wasn't widely known or accepted as a legitimate art form, however, until 1912, when Picasso and Braque introduced Paris to their works of cut, torn, and pasted paper. Before long, the bits of newspaper and wallpaper used to create still-life forms led to the inclusion of other common materials like matchbook covers and tobacco wrappings.

Of course, the term "collage" originated in France. It comes from the French word *coller,* which means "to glue." The names of many of the techniques that collage artists incorporate into their work today also have their roots in French. A few of the more well-known terms include

- *Découpage.* A collage of cut paper.
- *Frottage.* Rubbing to create a textured paper for collage.
- *Fumage.* Creating patterns by smoking paper.
- *Photomontage.* Using cut photographs to create a collage.

Many more techniques, including all of the paper-decorating techniques covered on pages 36–113, can be used to make collage materials. Although our focus is on paper collage, it's fun to include other materials, such as string, wire, cloth, feathers, or beads. Images can be representational, abstract, purely decorative, humorous, or deliberately confrontational—designed to make a social comment.

The choice of materials and the way you overlap and arrange them is totally up to you. Your collage can be centered around a particular idea or theme, or it can be a playful abstract piece unified by the repetition of a particular color or shape. Try not to get too serious if this is your first experience with collage; relax and have fun. If you really can't come up with an idea, consider following in the footsteps of the 20th-century artist Jean Arp, who designed one of his collages by letting pieces of paper fall at random to determine their position.

To get started, you'll need the following materials and equipment:

- *Decorative papers.* Papers that have been batiked, marbled, stenciled, stamped, dyed, or embellished in any way are great for collage. Look over the decorative papers you've produced and cut a few to begin a collage. You might also design some embossed or cast papers specifically for use in collage work.
- *Purchased papers.* Japanese papers, exotic handmade sheets, foils, lace papers, origami papers, commercial art and printing stock, corrugated papers, and wrapping papers are all good collage materials.

- *Found papers.* Wallpaper, printed sheet music, blueprints, airline boarding passes, old maps, posters, playbills, junk mail, tags, tickets, stamps, labels, calendar pages, magazine pages, postcards, old artworks—anything that can be recycled into collage material—can be saved in your "found paper" file (which can quickly become a found paper trunk). Many found papers, like newsprint, are highly acidic and tend to deteriorate quickly. If you seal them by coating them on both sides with matte medium you can prevent their demise. Coating papers with matte medium also renders them more fade-resistant.
- *Photographic materials.* Old photos that didn't turn out well, or shots of people or places you'd like to commemorate in a somewhat disassembled fashion, can be used in a photomontage. Cutting photos into strips and rearranging them can form interesting abstract designs. (And make a social comment.) Slides, negative strips, and contact sheets also make good collage materials.
- *Other collage materials.* String, wire, beads, feathers, leather, fabric, wire mesh, tape, shells, and other items can be added to a paper collage. Just be sure the materials aren't too heavy for your backing and that you don't include anything that will deteriorate or attract insects. (Unless, of course, you're into flypaper collage.)
- *Cutting tools.* Various types of scissors (including those that cut a decorative or deckle edge), X-Acto knives, and paper punches can be used to cut paper for collages. A ruler is helpful for cutting and tearing them.

Janet Hofacker describes her collaged artists books as "scavenger art." Many of her works are comprised of junk mail and paper found lying in city streets.

All kinds of found, handmade, and hand-decorated papers are suitable for collage.

- *Colors.* Colored pencils and various water-based paints, inks, and markers can be used to shade and color collage papers or parts of a collage. Pearlescent or iridescent inks and acrylics are especially fun to use.
- *Misting bottle.* This is helpful for delivering water to keep colors flowing when applying a watercolor or ink wash.
- *Glues.* If the papers used in your collage are lightweight, acrylic matte medium can be used to glue them down. A white glue like Sobo can also be used, although it tends to wrinkle lightweight papers. I use "Yes" paste in many of my collages because it won't wrinkle paper and isn't highly acidic. Avoid rubber cement—it bleeds through papers in just a few years and will ruin your collage. Other ways of attaching collage papers include using adhesive release paper and dry-mount tissue in a dry-mount press.
- *Brushes.* Large and small watercolor brushes are useful for applying water to help tear papers and give them a deckle edge. Brushes can also be used to enhance a collage surface by applying an ink wash to create a textured background. Brushes are also necessary for applying adhesives to collage materials.
- *Backing.* The support paper or backing board on which the collage materials are glued should be sturdy enough to support them without bending or buckling. Mat board, 140-lb. watercolor paper, foamcore board, or illustration board are often used for this purpose.

"Loving the Rose," a mixed-media collage by Jocelyn Curry, 13 × 8 inches (33 × 20.3 cm). Calligraphy, spattering, stamping, and colored pencil enhance the underlying collage work.

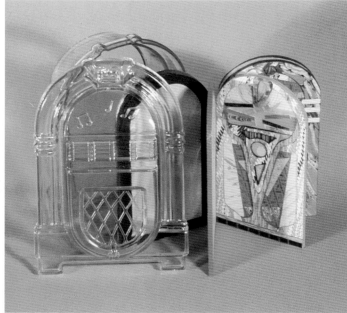

Edward Hutchins's works are often playful. This book, "Jukebox Quilts," contains seven cut-paper collages based on the jukebox designs of the 1930s and 1940s. It measures 5 × 3¹/₂ × 2 inches (12.7 × 8.9 × 5.1 cm).

- *Paper or plastic to cover work surfaces.* Recommended (but not essential) for protecting surfaces from ink stains and damage from glues.
- *Scrap paper.* Scrap paper is used and discarded as collage materials are glued. Freezer wrap or waxed paper can be used to cover glued papers as they are pressed flat.
- *Polaroid camera.* This is optional, but really helpful if you're creating a complicated work. It's frustrating to spend a lot of time positioning collage pieces and then find that you've lost track of their placement during the gluing process.

TEXTURING AND ALTERING PAPERS

Various design elements such as shape, texture, color, and line are important in a collage work. By texturing and altering collage papers, you can increase your palette and help keep your work exciting.

Tear or cut papers into large and small pieces, varying the shapes. The shapes can be geometric or organic, with hard or soft edges. Crumple papers to give them more dimension and texture. Wet and roll small bits of paper to add egg- and seedlike structures to a work. For more texturing options, peel back parts of papers that have been glued together, or sand them to expose their inner layers.

Tear a piece of paper away from you to give it a clean but ragged edge, or tear toward you to create an edge that features the paper's core. Lay down a line of water with a wet brush, let the water soak in, then pull the paper apart to create another type of deckle edge. Straight lines can be made by folding the paper first or by using a metal rule as a guide, but letting a water-filled brush wander over a paper can also be effective. (Don't use this technique with decorative papers that will be harmed by water or are embellished with any water-based media.) Use scissors that give a deckle, scalloped, or other decorative edge to paper—pinking shears aren't the only option anymore.

Give your papers a decorative edge by cutting them with edging scissors, tearing them, or wetting them with a paint brush and pulling them apart.

Cut thin, straight, or curved strips of paper, or roll sheets of paper into tubes to create linear structure within a work. Sometimes a predominantly horizontal collage needs a few vertical or diagonal lines to provide contrast and give it energy. Dip string in paper pulp to create paper-covered flexible lines for collage use.

COLORING COLLAGE PAPERS

Colored pencils, markers, inks, and paints can also be used to draw lines, emphasize the exposed edge of a torn sheet, and otherwise embellish collage papers. Inks and watercolor paints are great for coloring and texturing base papers on which other collage materials are glued. The plastic-wrap and salt techniques covered in chapter 2 (see pages 65 and 67, respectively) are ideal ways to produce base papers for collage.

CREATING DESIGNS

Collage is a broad term, and there are no hard-and-fast rules for assembling collage materials. Your collage can be abstract, decorative, or representational. You can overlap as few or as many papers as desired, using a monochromatic or varied color scheme. Let your intuition guide you as you move papers around, then examine your successful and unsuccessful placements to get a feeling for what seems to work and what doesn't.

Novices often worry that their first collages will be a mad jumble of papers. Working in just a few colors can usually prevent this from happening. Even strictly monochromatic collages, in which light and dark values of a single color are played against each other, are often very successful.

Experiment by moving materials to different positions and rotating them to create horizontal or vertical structures. Repeat shapes and color to keep a viewer's eye moving throughout a piece, but offer some contrast (horizontal lines in a vertical piece, an unexpected rough texture, or a flash of intense color) to keep the work from becoming monotonous.

When you feel you have a well-balanced composition that looks unified and finished, take a photograph if you have a Polaroid camera, then begin gluing the collage materials to their backing. (On some collages, I find it helpful to glue small overlapping elements to each other before gluing them to the collage support.)

PRESSING THE COLLAGE

Collages don't require any pressing unless lightweight backing materials begin to warp from being wet with glue or collage materials begin to curl. If this occurs, cover the collage with freezer wrap or waxed paper (to prevent any tacky glue from sticking) and press the collage under books or boards overnight.

VIEWING FINISHED WORK

It's interesting and sometimes very fruitful to get a small 5- × 7-inch (12.7- × 17.8-cm) windowed mat and use it to look at isolated parts of a collage. Frequently, a particular area will be striking while the collage as a whole is rather ho-hum. An artist friend routinely creates a large collage, then views it through a small mat and cuts the collage into smaller pieces, adding colored pencil and ink embellishments or other elements as needed.

FRAMING

Finished works with minimal relief can be matted and framed under glass. Foamcore board spacers can be used under mats to permit framing of paper collages with more dimension.

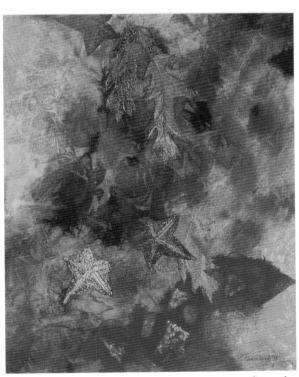

"Sylvan" by Rona Chumbook. Plastic-wrap printing forms the ideal background for this 14- × 11-inch (35.6- × 27.9-cm) mixed-media collage featuring rubber-stamped and embossed leaf cut-outs.

"Collage" by Shirley Siegenthaler. Opposing diagonal lines give this work, which measures 16 × 12 inches (40.6 × 30.5 cm), added interest.

Other Collage Techniques

Some collage artists borrow techniques from fiber art and tile work to create their paper constructions.

STITCHED COLLAGE

A number of paper artists, including Susan Kristoferson and Terri Fletcher, are producing exceptional stitched constructions by creating dyed, stenciled, or paste papers, then assembling them by sewing rather than gluing them together. On some works, feathers and beads are also either glued on or stitched in place. Artists like Arlene Gitomer start with handmade papers, then layer embroidery, beading, appliqué, and trapunto quilting techniques over them. The works pictured here rival anything I've seen done on fabric. If you're a quilter, or have some skill with a sewing machine, you may want to try working with paper to create a stitched collage.

"Prairie Coppice," a sewn paste-paper construction by Susan Kristoferson, 36 × 40³/₄ inches (91.4 × 103.5 cm).

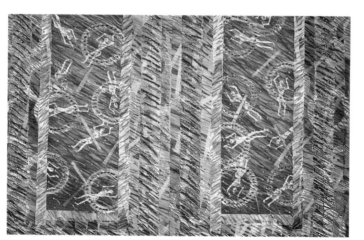

"Pearly Gates" by Terri Fletcher, 22 × 22 inches (55.9 × 55.9 cm). Materials for this shibori-dyed, stitched collage include vellum, paint, crayon, beads, and wood.

MOSAICS

Paper mosaics are distant relatives of the glazed tile work that originated in the Near East around 3000 B.C. In mosaic designs, papers are placed near each other but don't overlap as in traditional collage work. Often a background paper or mounting surface shows through an arrangement, mimicking the cement or plaster used in tile work. Many mosaic collages employ triangular-shaped papers. Others use small cut or torn squares or irregularly shaped pieces of paper to build a design.

The same supplies noted for traditional collage work can be used for mosaics. In addition, you'll probably want a pencil for sketching designs on your backing paper. Because you're working with small pieces of paper, it's easiest to plan out a mosaic design beforehand and then glue pieces in position as you fill in various parts. Otherwise, a sneeze or a visit by the studio cat could really ruin your day.

Decorative and colorful art papers can work together in a mosaic, especially if they are combined in a uniform color scheme. Pieces can be adhered in a haphazard fashion or follow the regular contours of a sketched design.

White glue, acrylic matte medium, or even a glue stick (for small pieces of paper) can be used as adhesives for paper mosaics. You can seal and protect a mosaic by applying a clear acrylic spray glaze in a gloss or matte finish. The gloss finish not only imparts a sheen to the work, but also mimics the glazes found in mosaic tile works.

"Quaker Crazy Quilt" by Sharon Schaich, 28 × 28 inches (71.1 × 71.1 cm). Purchased handmade papers arranged in mosaic designs form diamond shapes in this pieced paper quilt.

Papier-Mâché

Papier-mâché, a French term meaning "chewed paper," was coined in the 18th century to describe the process by which pulped paper and glue was transformed into a variety of decorative objects. Papier-mâché's beginnings, however, are much older. The craft began over a thousand years ago in China, where scraps of handmade paper were recycled into religious and ceremonial objects. The craft is still used to produce religious and ceremonial pieces and is especially prevalent in Asian and Mexican cultures. In the United States, it has long been used to create large, lightweight stage props and theatrical costumes, as well as giant heads and masks to be worn in parades and at carnivals.

Because it easily masquerades as metal, stone, and clay, papier-mâché is an ideal material for creating a number of smaller objects, too, like picture frames, bowls, and painted sculptures.

USING POWDERED PAPER PULP

Many craftspeople working with papier-mâché use a powdered paper pulp mixed with a glue binder (such as Celluclay) that handles like clay and dries with a hard finish. After being mixed with water, powdered paper pulp adheres to almost any surface and can be molded and sculpted easily. To experiment with this type of papier-mâché, you'll need:

- *Plastic table covering.* Papier-mâché is a messy technique, so protect your work surface before you start.
- *Papier-mâché supplies.* You'll need a large plastic freezer bag, water, plastic wrap, and a rolling pin to make the "dough," plus a plastic knife to cut it into pieces.
- *Newspaper and masking tape.* These are required for building an armature.
- *Petroleum jelly.* This is used as a release agent when working with papier-mâché over molds and other forms that will be removed.
- *X-Acto or craft knife.* You'll need one of these to remove unwanted features from a piece after it's dried.
- *Finishing supplies.* You may want to prime the finished piece with acrylic gesso, then use sandpaper to smooth its the surface before decorating it with acrylic paints.

Mixing Pulp and Water. Mix the powdered pulp with warm water a little at a time according to the manufacturer's directions. Knead the mixture in a plastic bag until no dry spots remain. (When properly mixed, it should be about the consistency of clay.) Sandwich a lump of the kneaded material between two sheets of plastic wrap and, using the rolling pin, roll the lump out until it's $1/8$ to $1/4$ inch (3 to 6 cm) thick. (It's as easy as pie.)

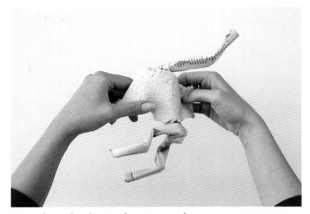

Mary Beth Ruby cutting the sections of rolled papier-mâché pulp into shapes.

Smoothing the sheets of papier-mâché onto an armature.

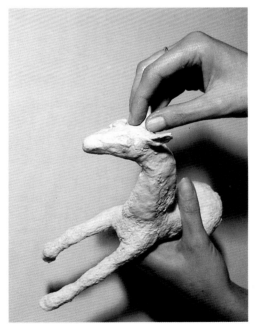

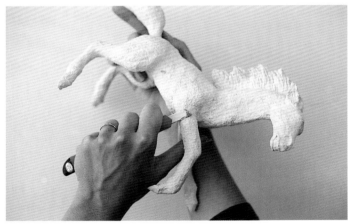

Using a craft knife to remove unwanted features from the dried form.

Using moistened fingers to help shape the papier-mâché form.

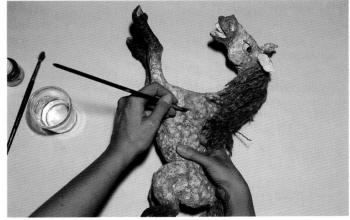

Painting the papier-mâché horse. All step-by-step photos by Paul D. Ruby

Covering a Form. When the papier-mâché mixture is rolled to an even thickness, it can be draped over a bowl or other rigid form without undercut areas. Grease the form with petroleum jelly so that it will release from the papier-mâché after it's dried. If necessary, use a plastic knife to cut sections of the rolled papier-mâché dough before wrapping it over a base support of wire and newspaper similar to that used by Mary Beth Ruby, whose papier-mâché techniques are shown on page 127.

LAYERED PAPIER-MÂCHÉ

The traditional papier-mâché method favored by craftspeople like Linda and John Beazley (whose "Pond Prince" is shown opposite) involves coating strips of torn paper with diluted white glue or wallpaper paste. Newspaper or handmade paper can be used, as well as a finishing layer of decorative paper. Thin colored paper or tissue can be layered over a form, and its color (and pattern, if it has one) can become a decorative focus in a work. Although tearing paper produces papier-mâché with a smooth, seamless finish, paper can also be cut into strips, with the resulting hard edges employed as part of the design. Layered papier-mâché is quite a bit more time-consuming than working with powdered pulp, as each layer of glue and paper must be dry before applying the next. Rushing the process can result in a moldy, weakened structure.

"Iguana in the Bathtub" by Mary Beth Ruby, a 9- × 18-inch (22.9- × 45.7-cm) sculpture made with pulped papier-mâché. Photo by Paul D. Ruby.

The dampened strips are then applied in multiple layers over removable molds such as woks and vases; permanent bases made from wire, wadded newspaper and masking tape, or cardboard structures; or disposable forms like balloons or eggs. Be sure to seal or grease forms with petroleum jelly, as needed. Mix water and wallpaper paste according to package directions; if using white PVA glue, dilute 3 parts glue with 1 part water. Tear or cut the paper (with the grain is easier) into strips or other shapes, then dip them in the paste or glue, removing any excess by running them through your fingers. For small pieces, it may be easier to brush the paste on.

"Pond Prince" by Linda and John Beazley, 8 × 8 inches (20.3 × 20.3 cm). This layered papier-mâché frog was formed out of wadded paper before being wrapped with paper soaked in wheat paste.

Begin layering the paper on the form, smoothing out any lumps or air bubbles as you work. Build up as many layers as needed, allowing each to dry before laying on the next. If you're creating a papier-mâché work that needs to be strong, like a table or tray, you'll have to apply up to twenty layers of paper. Applying layers in opposing directions can help build a sturdy structure. Delicate decorative bowls and ornaments, however, can be made in as few as three layers.

After 24 hours, remove the mold if the surface of the piece feels dry, then let the interior of the papier-mâché dry completely. This may take several days, depending upon how thick the papier-mâché is and how damp the weather is. NOTE: Drying time may be reduced by placing the work in the sun or in a warm oven for a short time. (Check on it periodically to be sure it doesn't burn.)

DRYING AND FINISHING

Once a papier-mâché object is thoroughly dry, the work can be sanded and sealed, if desired, to protect and strengthen it. It can also be given a coat of gesso primer to hide any exposed newsprint and prepare it for further painting or other decoration. Some craftspeople prime their work with gesso and sand it smooth before painting, stamping, or decorating it with blockprints. Others prefer the rougher texture of an unsanded piece.

Mary Beth Ruby creates a papier-mâché bowl of colored tissue by layering strips of it over a greased mold.

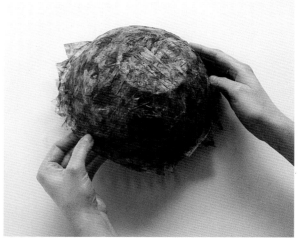

Because the bowl was coated with petroleum jelly, it easily releases the dried papier-mâché.

Contemporary Rolled Paper

Quilling is the art of rolling narrow strips of paper to form coiled shapes, which are then glued together to form intricate designs. The ends of the coiled papers may be left open to produce loose scrolls or glued in place to create closed coils, which can be pinched and bent between thumb and forefinger to create a variety of shapes, including tulips, leaves, and eyes. Quilling flourished during Victorian times, when young women covered inkstands, cribbage boards, and furniture with dainty quilled designs.

Some contemporary quilling, like the work of Mary Anne Landfield (see below), has so much dimension that it approaches paper sculpture (see page 152). Most quilled works maintain the original Victorian look, however, with floral themes still popular. Quilling techniques, of course, have changed. Instead of using bird quills, which were the original quilling tools, modern quillers use needles, toothpicks, or purchased quilling tools to support and roll their paper. Precut 1/8-inch-wide (3-mm-wide) quilling strips, sold in craft shops in a variety of colors, also make the craft less labor-intensive than it was in the past.

Loosely related to quilling, rolled-paper works, such as those made by Zack Vaughn (see page 132), are constructed by gluing rolled paper tubes to a mat board backing. The technique is simple. To try this kind of paper rolling, you'll need:

• *Paper.* Most any paper that's thin enough to roll will do.
• *X-Acto knife, metal-edged ruler, and cutting mat.* Run the blade against the edge of a metal ruler or a plastic ruler with a metal edge as you slice through the paper. Cut with the grain of the paper to assure that the strips roll smoothly.

Quilled cards by Mary Anne Landfield. By rolling fringed strips of paper, flower heads can be formed. Mary Anne often combines delicate quillwork with miniature paper sculpture.

- *Rolling device.* Large needles, pencils, or dowels can all be used as rolling tools. Thinner tools, of course, produce coils with smaller diameter centers.
- *White glue and glue applicator.* A white glue like Sobo holds rolled forms in place, joins rolled pieces, and attaches rolled designs to their backings. Use a glue brush for large areas and a toothpick where just a dot of glue is needed.
- *Waxed paper.* Working over waxed paper when applying glue to close a form or assemble rolled shapes will prevent designs from sticking to your working surface.
- *Acrylic sealer.* Spray finished works with an acrylic sealer to protect them.

Measure and cut several pieces of paper 3 × 5 inches (7.6 × 12.7 cm) wide. Roll each paper strip around a pencil or dowel to form a 3-inch (7.6-cm) tube. Apply glue to the end of the strip to glue it in place. When the glue is dry, remove the paper support.

Make a number of tubes of various sizes in colors that harmonize or in a monochromatic color scheme. Glue the tubes to a rigid box, picture mat, or other backing (perhaps previously covered with a similar decorative paper.) You can sketch out designs beforehand and cut and roll paper to fit, or work with a more serendipitous approach by creating designs from a number of tubes at hand. Finish with a spray coat of acrylic sealer.

ROLLED-PAPER BEADS

Rolled-paper beads can be made in a similar way by rolling paper around a weaving or knitting needle. Use long, thin triangular strips of plain or decorated paper and roll them, beginning with the wide end of the triangle. Apply dots of glue periodically as you roll the beads to keep the tapering rounds of paper in place. Glue the end of the triangle down; when it's dry, remove the beads and string them or use them in other projects, such as paper weavings.

Rolled-paper frames and boxes by Zack Vaughn.

To roll paper beads, cut long isosceles triangles and roll them around a weaving needle, beginning with the wide end. The black-and-white rolled-paper bead necklace pictured is by Carol McNally.

Cutting

Paper cutting began in China soon after the discovery of papermaking. A papercut showing twelve deerlike animals discovered in northern China in 1959 was probably created as early as A.D. 207. While the papercutting traditions of other countries and cultures are not as old as the Chinese, they too have long histories of the craft with established motifs and techniques passed on from one generation to the next. Religious symbols as well as animal and floral designs are often featured.

Paper-cutting techniques vary from region to region. In Mexico and Poland, for example, a single sheet of paper is often folded in half before being cut to produce a symmetrical pattern. In China, ten to twenty sheets of thin paper are stacked and pinned to a tray of wax before being cut as one. Paper-cutting tools vary as well. In Poland, the traditional tool of choice is bulky sheep shears. In China, a knife blade secured between strips of bamboo is often the preferred tool.

The weight of papers used for papercuts can range from heavy cardstock for nonfolded cuts to tissue-thin sheets for folded or stacked cutting. Images can be sketched on the paper before cutting, or designs can be cut on an accordion-folded sheet, paper-doll fashion, with the final image revealed to the cutter when the paper is opened. Colored paper may be used, or white paper may be cut and colored after the papercut is completed.

As you can see, the materials and equipment vary quite a bit, depending upon the type of paper cutting you do. Contemporary paper cutters, like Aric Obrosey, make use of even more equipment, employing electric drills and wood-burning tools to perforate and burn out parts of a design.

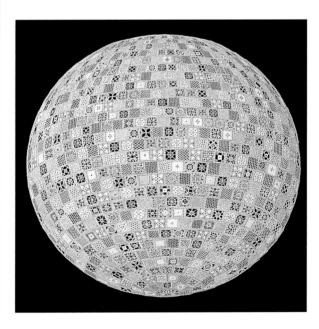

"Lace Disco Ball," burned-cut paper by Aric Obrosey, 29¼ inches (74.3 cm) in diameter.

RELIEF CUTS AND SURFACE TREATMENTS

Paper cutting can also be used to create relief textures in a sheet of paper. Instead of being made to remove parts of the sheet, relief cuts are designed to allow flaps of paper around a slit to be folded back. To try this type of cutting, you'll need:

- *Paper.* Work with heavy sheets of coverstock, like Canson or Strathmore papers.
- *Cutting tools.* Use a cutting mat or piece of glass as your cutting surface, and an X-Acto knife to make clean, sharp cuts.
- *A #2 pencil.* For sketching designs prior to cutting.
- *Metal ruler.* Used to align folds, cuts, and pencil lines.
- *Bone folder and awl.* For scoring and folding sheets.
- *Optional equipment.* You may want to use a graphic artist's template; a T-square, for lining up designs; or graph paper, for lining up repeat patterns.

Creating a Folded Structure. To produce a folded card or other freestanding structure, first determine the direction of the paper's grain. Then cut a piece of paper in the desired shape and size, making sure that the intended folds follow the grain. Score and fold the paper before making relief cuts.

Creating Relief Cuts. A series of Xs, triangles, curves, and parallel cuts, like those shown opposite, can be made at random or at measured intervals. When the resulting paper flaps are folded back, they create openings in the sheet of paper.

Use a pencil and ruler to draw designs on the back of your paper, or trace designs through a graphic artist's template. Cut through the lines drawn with an X-Acto knife, then fold back the flaps. If the paper is heavy, score the front of the sheet before attempting to fold the flaps. The relief design will be determined by the size of the slits and the degree to which you open the paper flaps. Place another decorative paper behind the openings, or let the subtle play of light and shadow on the folded areas remain the focus of the work.

REPEAT PATTERNS

By folding a sheet of paper before cutting it, you can create repeat patterns. A single fold produces a mirror image, while a double fold creates four identical designs. Intricate paper cuttings can be made by folding tissue-thin paper for as many as sixty-four repeats.

Additional materials needed for this type of paper cutting include thin text-weight Western or Oriental papers, large and small sharp scissors (including manicure scissors), and a paper punch. A piece of glass is easier to use than a cutting mat, as a smooth surface makes cutting easier.

Creating a series of parallel cuts in a sheet of paper. When the sheet is opened and every other cut is folded back, the card shown results.

A sheet of paper opened with a series of relief cuts. This technique is useful for making cards and creating surface texture on paper sculptures.

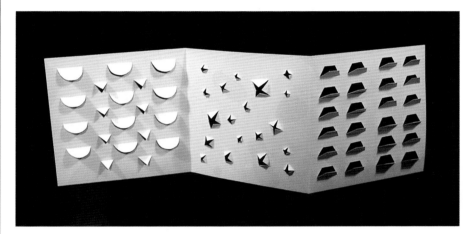

When using scissors to create repeat paper cuts, try to keep your cutting hand steady and turn the paper into the blades. To create the repeat cuts pictured, pieces of block-print paper 6 × 22 inches (15.2 × 55.9 cm) long were accordion-folded.

Fold a sheet of paper following one of the patterns shown below. Pencil in a design or cut one free-form, making sharp geometric cuts or smooth flowing ones. Cut without hesitation to avoid ragged edges. When using scissors, try to keep your cutting hand stable, turning the paper as you work. If using an X-Acto knife, make sure the blade is sharp and rotate the paper on the glass as you cut. Be sure to leave part of the folded edge intact so that designs remain joined.

Follow these basic folding patterns used to produce repeat paper cuts. Create your own designs or copy the cutting patterns suggested. Remember to always leave part of the folded edge intact so designs remain joined.

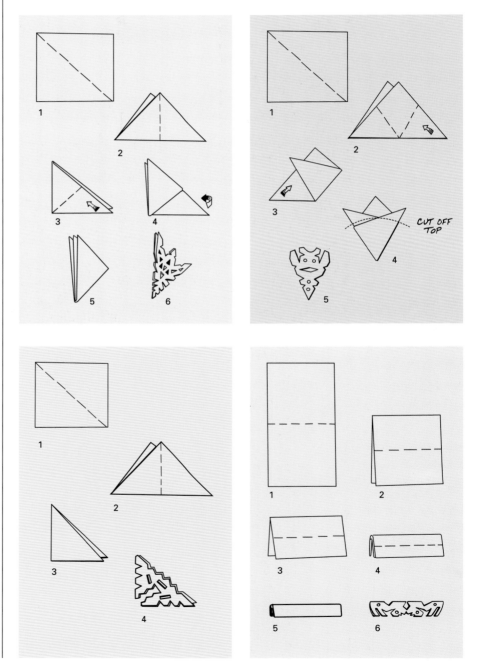

WORKING WITH A FLAT SHEET

Scissors, X-Acto knives, scalpels, rotating punches, and even electric drills can be used to cut designs into a flat sheet of paper. The complex lacey paper cut-outs of Aric Obrosey are made with a variety of tools. Here he describes the techniques used to create "Detritus Doily":

> I began with a piece of Arches Cover Black, which was cut from a roll and flattened by wetting and taping to a board. Next, an elaborate drawing was done directly onto the paper using white charcoal pencil. I then cut the image out, perforating different areas with different tools to achieve varying effects; an X-Acto knife for some, a Dremel bit and drill for others. Elsewhere a wood-burning tool was used, and in certain sections the paper was perforated with a sharp stylus and then torn away.

"Detritus Doily," cut paper by Aric Obrosey, 51 × 48 inches (129.5 × 121.9 cm).

COLORING PAPERCUTS

A variety of paper-decorating techniques can be used to create papers for specific paper-cutting projects. When I created the papers for "Secret Garden," I chose a marbled design that suggested leaves and vines. Anne-Claude Cotty's vibrant paste designs were also intended to portray the foliage and creatures that animate her artist's books.

The intricate *Scherenschnitte* papercuts by Sandra Gilpin are also colored before the cutting is done. Sandra draws and then paints her designs with watercolors in hues that lend an antique feeling, reflecting the Pennsylvania-German tradition of the craft. After the paints are dry, Sandra begins cutting, using an X-Acto knife and surgical and manicure scissors.

Some paper cuts, like those made from thin tissue and cut in multiples, may be colored after the cuts are made. In China, a dye is applied to a stack of cut designs and allowed to soak through to the bottom sheet. Scissor-cut repeat designs can also be colored after they're cut by applying dyes to the cut edges with a small paint brush.

Some of Aric Obrosey's cut-outs are colored as he works. The sepia tone of "Lace Disco Ball" (page 133) is a result of the wood-burning tool he used to create the piece.

"Secret Garden," layered and cut marbled paper by Diane Maurer-Mathison, 15 × 13 inches (38.1 × 33 cm). A waved chevron marbled pattern was created for this work to suggest leaves.

Detail of "Tillandsia & Co./Curtain Calls" by Anne-Claude Cotty, 10 × 12 × 1 inch (25.4 × 30.5 × 2.5 cm). Vibrant paste-paper designs color Anne-Claude's artist's books.

"Variations on a Heart," a Scherenschnitte papercut by Sandra Gilpin, 9¹/₂ × 9¹/₂ inches (24.1 × 24.1 cm). Sandra uses an X-Acto knife and tiny scissors to create her intricate papercuts.

Weaving

Paper weaving is another ancient craft that originated in China soon after the invention of papermaking. It's a versatile papercraft that can be used to accent larger works or form an intricate matrix over another structure such as a box or cylinder. Woven paper screens and mats can also be created, as well as paper hangings and collages.

The simple over/under *tabby weave*, the mainstay of fiber weaving, offers even more design opportunities to paper weavers. When working with paper, you can alter the size and shape of the vertical *warp* strips as well as the horizontal filler *weft* strips—a simple matter of tearing or cutting them into different widths or patterns.

To explore paper weaving, you'll need the following basic materials:
- *Paper.* Heavy-or medium-weight paper can be used for the warp; any weight paper for the weft. Decorative papers or photos can be used, as well as white or colored plain stock.
- *Other supplies.* You'll also need a cutting mat, an X-Acto knife, a metal ruler, and a pencil.

BASIC TABBY WEAVE

Using a sharp X-Acto knife and a metal ruler, cut parallel vertical lines in an 8- × 10-inch (20.3- × 25.4-cm) sheet of paper. Leave a 1-inch (2.5-cm) margin at the top and bottom of the sheet. These vertical strips of paper make up the warp. Now cut loose strips from another contrasting piece of paper that's about 10 inches (25.4 cm) long. These are your weft strips.

"Woven Box" by Myrna Bendett, 8 × 8 × 4 inches (20.3 × 20.3 × 10.2 cm). Myrna's meticulous paste-paper weavings often feature strips of paper with decorative cut edges.

Begin weaving the weft strips over and under the paper warp, letting the ends extend on either side. Begin the second row by going under and then over the warp strips. After the weaving is completed, the weft ends as well as the warp margins can be trimmed off, or left ragged as part of the design.

Altering the Warp

Although it's easiest to weave with the warp strips held stationary by paper margins, warp strips can also be held taut by using masking tape to attach them to a working surface or gluing them in place on a backing sheet. Both options allow the warp strips to be spread out, creating openings or negative space in the weave.

Warp strips can be altered to add more interest to a weaving. Instead of cutting straight strips, try tearing them, or cutting them in a zig-zag or curved pattern. Use decorative-edge scissors to produce strips with a pinked, scalloped, deckle, or notched appearance. (You could also create thin strips of handmade paper to incorporate authentic deckle edges.) A paper punch is handy for making notched strips. Thin strips of paper can also be woven in and out between punched holes to create a woven warp. Very thin paper can be spun into a warp by rolling and twisting it between your fingers to create stringlike paper threads instead of flat warp strips.

A paper weaving being made on a zig-zag warp employing the basic tabby over/under pattern. By altering the size and shape of the warp or weft, interesting but simple weaving variations can be achieved. The zig-zag cut paper beside the weaving was traced several times to create a pattern for the warp.

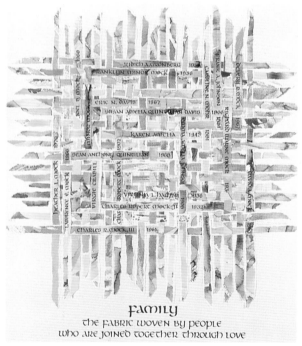

FAMILY
the fabric woven by people
who are joined together through love

"A Celebration of Family," copyright © by Karen A. Brown, 26 × 30 inches (66 × 76.2 cm). By diverting from the tabby weave and using multicolored warp and weft strips, Karen creates exceptional weavings of words, colors, and papers.

Altering the Weft

Weft strips can be altered in much the same way as the warp. The weft can be monochromatic, or vary in color from row to row. The weft can be linear or curved, cut or torn, and wide or narrow. Paper beads can be added to a warp to further enhance a work.

Another way to alter the weft and change the appearance of woven paper is to divert from the tabby-weave pattern. Try weaving over two warp strips and under one, or devise another weaving configuration. You'll be amazed at the variety of designs that can be created.

THREE-DIMENSIONAL WEAVING

If many thin, long weft strips are woven into just a few warp strips, a relief design will result. The strips can fall forward on their own, or be bent and braided together.

Another way to create dimension is to pull loops of weft up from the back of the weaving. Small dowels might also be inserted as you work and removed when the weft is in place. The resulting loops can be left as is or pinched into triangular shapes.

Freestanding paper weavings can be made by scoring and accordion-pleating heavy paper, then opening it out to cut warp slits in appropriate places. The weft can appear and disappear throughout a piece to create a fascinating woven paper sculpture.

Freestanding paper weavings are easy to make by cutting warp slits in heavy folded paper and weaving paper strips through the openings.

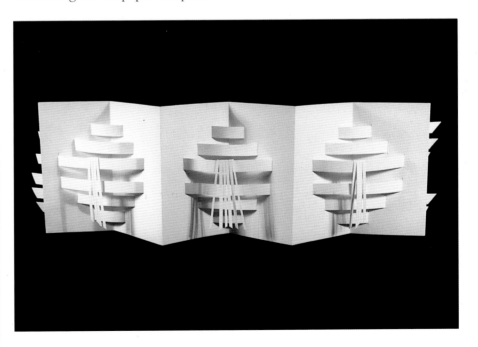

Pleating

Although paper pleating or folding has been mentioned throughout this book as a preliminary step to orizomegami (see page 84) and paper cutting (page 133), pleating is worth a closer look. It's a great way to create freestanding structures for paper weaving (page 139), as well as folded notecards, pages for handmade books, and pleated fans or medallions to be used as accents on larger works. Well known as an origami technique, folding gives paper additional strength. Light and shadow play off the planes of a pleated structure, lending drama to it. Materials and equipment include:

- *Paper.* Depending upon the structure being created, light-, medium- or heavyweight paper in white or colors may be called for.
- *Other supplies.* A cutting mat, an X-Acto knife and scissors, a metal ruler, a scoring tool, a bone folder, glue, and a glue brush.

BASIC CARD FOLDS

Simple card folds include single horizontal and vertical folds. A *French fold* is made by folding a paper in half horizontally and then vertically. A *gatefold* is made by folding (or scoring and folding) a sheet of paper one-fourth of the way in from either edge. The card is closed by folding each gate toward the center of the card to hide the surprise inside. Of course, cards needn't be square or rectangular, or folded in a traditional fashion. All kinds of liberties can be taken with cards, folding them at odd angles to create a kind of puzzle for the recipient.

"If All the World" by Jan Owen. The pleating in the center of Jan's handmade book, which measures 23 × 24¹/₂ × 8 inches (58.4 × 62.2 × 20.3 cm), forms the perfect support for the paper strips that spring from them.

ACCORDION-PLEATED STRUCTURES

Accordion pleats can be used to create expanding cards or pages for handmade books. You can overlap and glue pleated sections together to make longer folded pages. Remember to check for grain direction, then fold, or score and fold, turning the paper as you work, using the previous fold as a guide to create equidistant mountain and valley folds.

The tops of accordion-pleated pages can be cut in a decorative design suggesting a cityscape, or cut in gentle curves resembling hills, lower in front, growing taller toward the back pages. Either would be a perfect base for further collage work.

Narrow pleating can be used to produce decorative fans. After sharpening the creases with a bone folder, gather and glue the base of the pleated structure together. You could also stitch or wrap the base to hold the pleats in place. If some of the finished fold-and-dye papers are gathered into pleats and bound in the center with a band of paper, another type of fan or a structure resembling a fish can be made.

To make a circular medallion, accordion-pleat a long strip of paper, glue the first and last pleats together to make a loose cone, then flatten the structure and glue it to a backing sheet, weighting it with a book until dry.

An assortment of pleated forms, including an oil-marbled double medallion and a suminagashi-marbled, reverse-pleated wing. The fan and fish were made by gathering and binding papers created with simple fold-and-dye techniques.

REVERSE-PLEATED STRUCTURES

A type of reverse-pleated structure reminiscent of art deco designs can be made by folding a square piece of paper in half to form a triangle, and accordion-pleating the triangle, beginning at its base. (If this is your first attempt at reverse pleating, a thin but crisp sheet of computer paper would be good to start with.) When the triangle is accordion-pleated, bend all the folds in the opposite direction. This action indents each crease from both sides so the paper will move into mountain and valley folds more easily as you manipulate it.

Now open out the paper and begin forming the final structure, pinching the first set of fold lines into mountain folds while pushing the second set back into valley folds. The third set will begin to rise into mountain folds as you push the fourth set into valley folds. The paper will begin to collapse in on itself along the center fold as you work.

When all the pleats are in place, collapse the work along the center fold. Use a bone folder to sharpen the pleats and help maintain their proper position. Then open the work out to see the final structure. Reverse-pleated works can also be made from heavier paper if you rescore every other fold line on opposite sides of the paper to allow the mountain and valley folds to be formed.

A variation of this pleated form resembling a wing is shown on pages 117 and 143. To create the winglike structure, begin with a triangular piece of paper. Fold it in half to form a second triangle, then follow the remaining instructions for making reverse-pleated structures.

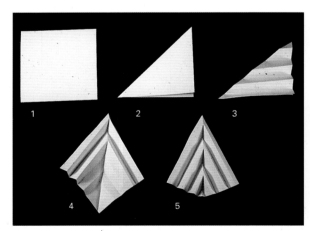

The steps involved in creating the art deco reverse-pleated structure. (1) A square piece of paper (2) is folded in half to create a triangle. (3) The triangle is accordion-pleated starting at its base, then all the pleats are folded in the opposite direction. (4) The paper is opened and (5) the final mountain and valley folds are pinched and pushed into place.

Pinching the mountain-fold pleats to create the art deco reverse-pleated form.

Pop-Ups

Commercial pop-up books have been available since the 19th century, when a London publisher added three-dimensional surprises to a line of children's stories. Later in the century, German publishers added even more sophisticated pop-up devices to their books. The trend was slow to reach American publishers; it wasn't until the 20th century that the books really caught on in the United States.

Many contemporary book and paper artists like Carol Barton, known for her playful artist's books, are exploring *pop-ups,* which consist of paper activated by opening and closing a fold, and *fold outs,* which require a reader's physical participation. A good place to experience pop-up designs is in the children's book department of a large bookstore, where you'll find titles that transform themselves into whole villages if you lift and crease a few pages. Two particularly exciting books, *The Ultimate Ocean Book* and *The Ultimate Bug Book* (both published by Golden Books), contain pop-ups engineered by James Roger Diaz. Not only do these books offer lots of design inspiration, but they're bound to turn anyone back into a wide-eyed kid again.

Pop-ups are supposed to be fun—for the paper artist as well as the viewer. But many people are intimidated by the thought of trying to create a pop-up, mainly because of all the measuring required. And the truth is that if measurements and folds are off in a pop-up card or book, it will show. If you have to keep handling a paper to figure out which folds to push in, and which to bring forward, that, too, will be evident in the finished piece. For this reason, it's best to design prototypes of simple pop-ups on inexpensive graph paper first, so you can determine where to cut and how to fold before you make the finished work on stiffer, more expensive paper.

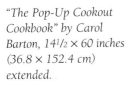

"The Pop-Up Cookout Cookbook" by Carol Barton, 14^1/$_2$ × 60 inches (36.8 × 152.4 cm) extended.

To begin playing with pop-ups, buy an inexpensive graph paper tablet laid out with four squares to 1 inch (2.5 cm). With a sheet of graph paper and a pair of scissors you can create pop-ups in minutes—without measuring a thing.

To make a step or a pop-up support for a paper cut-out, just fold a sheet of graph paper in half and make two slits near the center of the sheet. The slits on the example shown opposite, top, are seven blocks deep and a couple of inches apart. Cut on a line and be sure to end each cut at the bottom of the same square so that your slits are even and parallel. Fold and crease the flap of paper you just created along the dotted line as shown, which connects the base of each slit. Move it backward, then forward, to crease it in both directions.

Now open your folded paper enough to push the flap through to the other side and flatten it. The top of the flap, which was originally a mountain fold, will become a valley fold. (Your paper will look like the second step in the illustration opposite, top, when the paper is flat.) Use a bone folder to sharpen the creases. Now open the paper to see a little step, which when made on heavier paper can be used as a pop-up support for a picture, drawing, or photograph.

To make two more steps, cut two more slits, each two blocks in from the first two. Make these about three blocks deep and follow the same procedure to fold the paper in both directions and push the flaps through. Your paper will look like the second part of the illustration shown opposite, center, when it's flat. When opened, it will sport three steps or ledges that, when made of heavier paper, can be decorated with drawings or collage work.

To create an interesting pop-up with multiple slits that needs no further embellishment, copy the one shown opposite, bottom. To crease it, bend each flap forward, then backward, before opening the paper and pulling each flap to the front. Then close the paper again and crease the flaps into their final positions.

TRANSFERRING THE DESIGN TO HEAVY PAPER

Cardstock (the best choice for crisp designs) or a coverstock like Canson Mi-Teintes are good papers to use for final work. The papers are thin enough to crease with light scoring and sturdy enough to hold the crease. To transfer your graph-paper pop-up to heavier paper (without measuring) just lay the slit design over heavy paper, making sure that fold lines run cross-grain. Although this runs contrary to the standard rules of working with paper grain (see page 116), it helps produce pop-ups that hold their shape. Mark the end of each cut with a pinprick, align a metal ruler with the marks, then cut parallel slits. You can use your graph paper as a pattern over and over again. NOTE: When working with very heavy paper, you will need to score the base of each flap before attempting to crease and push it through to the front.

The finished single pop-up shelf and graph-paper practice sheets showing (1) where to cut and fold and (2) how the sheet looks when the shelf flap is pushed through.

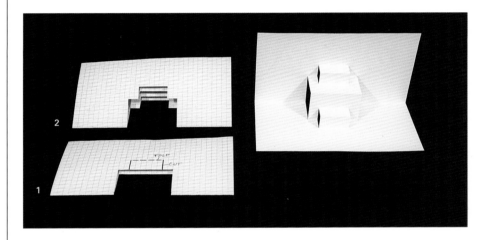

The finished triple pop-up shelves and graph-paper practice sheets showing (1) where to cut and fold and (2) how the sheet looks when the second set of shelves is pushed through.

The multiple-slit pop-up design and its graph-paper practice pattern.

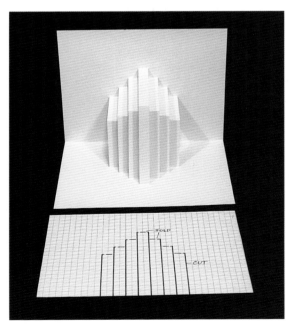

CREATING A BACKING

To create a backing for a freestanding pop-up or a pop-up card that won't bind when you attempt to fold the card, cut a piece of cardstock slightly shorter and narrower than your pop-up. (This step might have to be measured.) Cut the paper backing in half and glue each half to the pop-up, letting the fold line extend. Be sure to keep glue off the parts of the structure that are meant to rise, or they won't be able to operate. Glue cut-outs to pop-up supports, if desired, or enjoy the work for its structure alone. Multiple-slit pieces can be enjoyed in a horizontal or vertical direction.

CREATING A WIDE-MOUTHED OPENING

One of the most popular and simplest pop-up designs is pictured in Jan Owen's *Little Fish* book. To make this structure, lightly draw or trace a triangle on the back of a folded paper and slit it from its base to its apex, as shown opposite, top, to create two triangles. Fold each of these on the lines indicated, creasing them forward and then backward on the same fold lines. Then open the paper slightly and push each triangle through to the front of the sheet. Close the sheet, sharpen the creases, and open the paper to see the mouths pop up.

Experiment with these simple techniques, altering the angle of your slits to make asymmetrical pop-ups as well as symmetrical ones. Once you understand how they're formed, you can begin altering the shape of the slits, too, to increase your design options.

"Little Fish" by Jan Owen, calligraphy and gouache on paste paper, 5 × 10½ inches (12.7 × 26.7 cm).

Two little wide-mouthed paste-paper creatures and the practice sheets showing (1) where to cut and fold the paper, (2) how the paper looks when the triangles are folded forward, and (3) how the paper looks when the triangle mouth is pushed through. Note how the smaller figure, created against the grain of the paper, holds the pop-up mouth better.

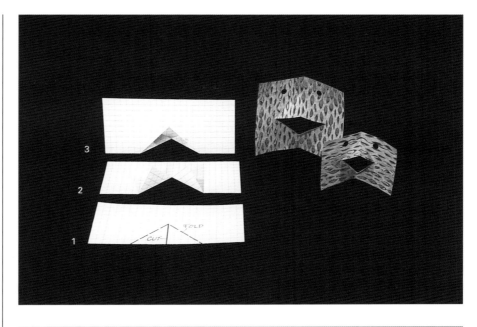

"Rhythmic Notes on 7 Folds" by Carol Barton, 9 × 58 inches (22.9 × 147.3 cm) extended. Carol used spray paint on paper printing plates to create the unusual offset-printed designs.

Follow the instructions and photos contributed by artist and author Shereen LaPlantz (see pages 150 and 151) to learn some of her favorite pop-up techniques. She created the delightful pop-up paper dollhouse especially for this book. Although the slit-and-tab construction does require accurate measuring, if you work slowly and carefully the results will be worth the effort. Besides, now that you've made a few pop-ups, you shouldn't need your graph-paper training wheels anymore.

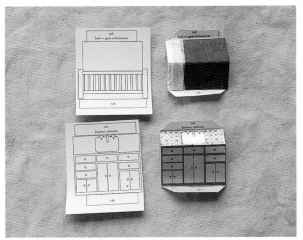

Shereen describes the process of creating her pop-up book: "I drew the outlines of the doors, windows, closets, furniture, and other elements in PageMaker and printed it on the paper that serves as the house walls (Beckett Cambric Cover). I painted or collaged in the wall treatments, then cut them to size; I also cut the tabs that slip through slits in the floor and are glued to its underside. Since this house is in the Craftsman's Style (also called a bungalow), I cut 'wood veneer' from very sheer paper to make the doors, cabinets, furniture, and moldings."

"Furniture is generally a rectangle dressed up to look like furniture. I drew these elements on heavy paper. Tabs are necessary to adhere the furniture to both the wall and the floor, so I cut tabs both above and below each piece. To make the bed, I used rice paper for both layers of sheets and for the blankets. Remember that rooms and furniture must fold flat in order for the book to close, so nothing can be bulky."

"At this point, I glued and adhered the walls together, measured the exact height of the furniture on the walls, and made a slit in the wall to match the width of the furniture. Precision is critically important if the pop-up furniture is to actually pop-up—and also lie flat when the book is closed."

"I cut the archway between the living room and kitchen after the two walls were glued together, taking care not to make the opening too close to the top edge, which would make the wall weak. I then measured the space between the outer edges of the walls to calculate the size of the squares for the floor."

"To create the floor, I folded the paper like an origami water bomb. (Fold a square of paper in half in both directions, turn it over, then fold in half diagonally.) I cut slits into the floor along the fold lines as shown before painting or collaging on the floor treatments, making sure that the wall tabs fit into each of the floor slits. I then made the floor slits for each piece of furniture by measuring the width of the furniture, then making a slit the same distance from the wall—EXACTLY. Mismeasurements mean the furniture will not pop up correctly."

"CRITICAL: Even if the furniture requires it, the floor slit CANNOT extend over the center fold line. If the furniture requires it (like the kitchen sink), notch out the floor tab so it doesn't interfere with the center fold line."

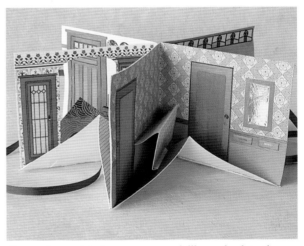

"The opposite problem occurs when something is positioned too close to the outside edge, so that the furniture must extend past the floor's edge. Leave some space between the slit and the floor's outer edge for stability. If necessary, trim the floor tab until it fits the allotted space. When creating tabs, consider stability first, then take into account how easily they will allow the book to be opened and closed. Slip each wall's and the furniture's floor tabs through the appropriate slits and glue them in place. Be very precise."

Shereen's completed pop-up paper dollhouse book in the process of closing.

Sculpture

If you've experimented with some of the papercraft techniques shown in this chapter, you've already learned most of the basics needed to produce paper sculpture. In fact, you may have already made some paper sculptures. By creasing, scoring, pleating, folding, and making relief cuts in a sheet of paper, you've already transformed paper from a flat plane into a three-dimensional form with convex and concave surfaces—in short, into sculpture.

If you crumpled an unsuccessful project (probably the reverse-fold structure shown on page 144) into a ball to toss it into the wastebasket, you created another sculptural form with lots of peaks and valleys. (Although paper sculpture dates back to the 1700s in England, crumpled sculpture probably occurred before then.)

By learning a few more techniques, you'll be able to roll, curl, and shape paper into three-dimensional curved structures. These new techniques will allow you to create a greater variety of abstract and representational pieces that, with the help of white glue, tabs and slits, and a little imagination, can be assembled into a paper sculpture. Materials and equipment include:

- *Paper.* Medium- and heavyweight papers, like Canson Mi-Teintes, Strathmore charcoal paper, watercolor paper, coverstock, and Canford Papers, can be used.
- *Cutting tools.* You'll need a cutting mat, an X-Acto knife with several #11 blades (a second knife with a dull blade can be helpful), and scissors.
- *Paper-curling devices.* A wooden dowel and bone folder are fine.
- *Gluing supplies.* Apply white glue with a glue brush and toothpicks.
- *Foamcore board (optional).* This is used to raise layers or elements of a sculpture.

Experiment with creating three-dimensional curved shapes by using an X-Acto knife to cut out an elongated S shape from a piece of heavy paper, making sure the S follows the grain of the paper. Then use an X-Acto knife with a dull blade or the point of a pair of scissors to score the cut-out, following the curve down the S's center. (You can also try scoring the cut-out with the same blade you used to cut the S, but apply minimal pressure to avoid cutting completely through the paper.)

Now create a mountain fold, using your fingers to bend the sheet away from the scored line. The resulting form will be a curved shape with angular flat planes that catch and reflect the light. Multiples of this shape could become waves in a paper seascape.

Cut out another, wider piece of paper, and try scoring two lines in it—one on the front of the sheet to be bent into a mountain fold, and one on the reverse side of the sheet to become a valley fold. Now try slicing out more narrow, slightly curved pieces of paper that taper to a point. Score and fold these to create structures that resemble grass or leaves. Although you may be tempted to try cutting shapes with scissors, long, gentle curves can be cut most accurately with a sharp X-Acto knife.

To practice creating curled paper that might represent flower tendrils, hair curls, or a pig's tail, cut out a long strip of paper with the grain running across it and roll it over the edge of a bone folder as though you're curling a ribbon for a gift package. Now roll an identical piece of paper around a dowel to see how that influences curl. The curl can be further shaped by rolling it with your fingers to tighten it, or by pulling the paper to open it.

To create a circular or oval dimensional shape, cut out a paper circle or teardrop shape and slit it to its center. Overlap the edges and glue one edge over the other to create a structure that might become a flower petal, an animal ear, fish scales, or a horseshoe crab shell.

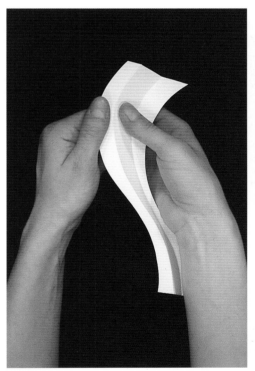

Bending the scored paper away from the fold line to form a mountain fold.

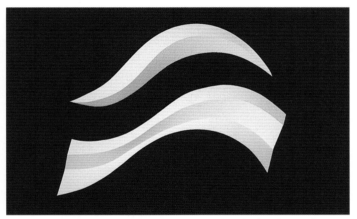

The angular flat planes of three-dimensional curved and scored paper catches and reflects the light.

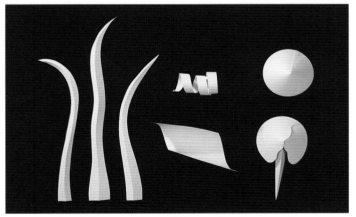

Scored and curled papers that could be used as elements of paper sculptures.

Much can be learned by cutting out different shapes and bending or curling them, and by examining other paper sculptors' work and working methods. "Sun Image" by Hal Lose was constructed by slicing smooth flowing cuts into a Canson paper circle. Both the top and the bottom of the circle were opened to add more dimension to the face. The ends of the marbled sun's flare were bent and curled with a bone folder to help them reflect light and shadow. (Hal sometimes uses a clothes steamer to relax a paper enough to make complex curves, which the paper maintains after it dries.)

Sometimes paper sculptors curl tiny pieces of paper with their fingers to create a work. Hal Lose's crab, shown below, right, both assembled and in separate pieces that each suggest a part of the crab's anatomy, was created this way.

The precise cutting and finishing evident in Hal's work can be seen again in "Sandwich Man" (opposite). The outer edge of each cut has been rubbed with an etching tool to smooth any rough edges. Hal often scores his papers with a specially sharpened tooth-cleaning tool.

"Sun Image" by Hal Lose, 18 inches (45.7 cm) in diameter. Both the rich color and the pattern of the marbling add to this work.

Hal Lose's crab, assembled and broken down into its separate elements, each suggestive of a crab's anatomy.

Although a few paper sculptors use a knife as a drawing implement, most use lightly drawn pencil lines as guides to help them. Other sculptors glue or staple photocopies of drawings to their paper and cut through two layers of paper at once. That way they avoid having to erase pencil lines later on.

Hidden supports are often employed to connect and raise portions of the work to create shadow and give added dimension to the sculpture. Hal used pieces of foamcore to raise layers of the sun sculpture. Other artists use four-ply matboard, foam tape, and even pieces of clear plastic for this purpose.

Hidden attachments, which are used to glue paper sculptures to a heavy watercolor paper backing board or other support, include paper tabs and loops (like those created for a paper chain). White glue is applied to one side of the loop and pressed against the backing, while the other side is glued to the back of the sculpture piece.

"Sandwich Man" by Hal Lose, 18 × 24 × 6 inches (45.7 × 60.9 × 15.2 cm).

Many paper sculptors have a favorite paper (some work almost exclusively on white Canson) but the subject of the sculpture will often dictate what paper should be used. Nancy Cook loves to work with Strathmore charcoal paper, which she used to create "Heron on the Bay" (below), because "it's strong and forgiving" when you bend and crease it. She again used charcoal paper to create the landscape for "Beauty Is in the Eye of the Beholder," but switched to stiffer, stronger Arches watercolor paper in different weights to create the outer structure for the eye.

"Heron on the Bay" by Nancy Cook, 8 × 10 inches (20.3 × 25.4 cm).

"Beauty Is in the Eye of the Beholder" by Nancy Cook, 11¹/₂ × 15 × 3 inches (29.2 × 38.1 × 7.6 cm).

The photos below show Nancy at work on a peony flower, a form comprised of many nested circular pieces. Her skills as a paper cutter and sculptor enable her to create a realistic work with fringed, scalloped, and curved petals alternating between flower layers. Nancy began the peony by making several drawings of the flower to get a "feel" for the piece. She then cut a number of circles from 100-percent rag Strathmore charcoal paper. These can be cut freehand or by using a compass. The sizes vary, as the interior layers of the flower must be smaller than the outer ones.

When Nancy has worked out her cutting design, she makes a template to use as a pattern for other layers of the flower. The petals can be sectioned and curved with fingers or the closed blades of a pair of scissors. Some are shaded with a colored pencil to help define the petal structure. The flower is assembled with small amounts of white glue applied with a toothpick, and finally glued in position on a bed of paper leaves.

Nancy Cook cutting one of the paper circles that will be transformed into peony petals for her flower sculpture.

Using the closed blades of a pair of scissors to shape the flower petals. Nancy sometimes uses just her fingers to give a slight curve to paper.

Colored pencils are used to accent and define finished flower petals.

The finished peony flower.

Further Reading

Barrett, Timothy. *Japanese Papermaking*. New York: John Weatherhill Inc., 1986.

Dawson, Sophie. *The Art and Craft of Papermaking*. Philadelphia: Running Press, 1992.

Guyot, Don. *An Introduction to Japanese Marbling*. Seattle: Brass Galley Press, 1988.

Heller, Jules. *Papermaking*. New York: Watson-Guptill Publications, 1978.

Hunter, Dard. *Papermaking: The History and Technique of an Ancient Craft*. New York: Dover Publications, Inc., 1978.

Jackson, Paul. *The Pop-Up Book*. New York: Henry Holt and Company, 1993.

LaPlantz, Shereen. *Cover to Cover*. Asheville, North Carolina: Lark Books, 1995.

Maile, Anne. *Tie and Dye As a Present Day Craft*. New York: Ballantine Books, 1971.

Masterfield, Maxine. *In Harmony with Nature*. New York: Watson-Guptill Publications, 1990.

Maurer, Diane Vogel. *Marbling: A Complete Guide to Creating Beautiful Patterned Papers and Fabrics*. New York: Friedman/Fairfax, 1994.

Maurer, Diane, and Paul Maurer. *An Introduction to Carrageenan & Watercolor Marbling*. Spring Mills, Pennsylvania: Hand-Marbled Papers, 1984.

Toale, Bernard. *Basic Printmaking Technique*. Worcester, Massachusetts: Davis Publications, 1991.

Ziegler, Kathleen, and Nick Greco. *Paper Sculpture*. Rockport, Massachusetts: Rockport Publishers Inc., 1994.

Source Directory

Listed at right are the suppliers for many of the materials used in this book. In general, a consumer's most convenient source for paper art supplies are local art supply and craft retailers. If you need something that they don't have in stock they will usually order it for you. When purchasing high-quality materials for techniques such as marbling and papermaking, however, it's best to deal with specialized suppliers who can answer technical questions.

Aiko's Art Materials Import, Inc.
3347 North Clark Street
Chicago, Illinois 60657
(312) 404-5600
Japanese papers and art supplies

Amsterdam Art
1013 University Avenue
Berkeley, California 94710
(510) 649-4800
Art supplies and papers

Carriage House Paper
P.O. Box 197
North Hatfield, Massachusetts 01066
(800) 669-8781
Papermaking supplies

Diane Maurer Hand-Marbled Papers
P.O. Box 78
Spring Mills, Pennsylvania 16875
(814) 422-8651
Marbling, paste paper, and Boku Undo dye supplies

Daniel Smith
4150 First Avenue South
P.O. Box 84268
Seattle, Washington 98124-5568
(800) 426-6740
Art supplies and papers

Dick Blick
P.O. Box 1267
Galesburg, Illinois 61402-1267
(800) 447-8192
Art supplies and papers

Dieu Donné Papermill, Inc.
433 Broome Street
New York, New York 10013-2622
(212) 226-0573
Papermaking supplies and papers

Dreamweaver Stencils
1910 Hardt Street
Loma Linda, California 92354
(909) 796-6002
Embossing and stenciling supplies

La Papeterie St. Armand
950 Rue Ottawa
Montreal, Quebec
Canada H3C 1S4
(514) 874-4089
Papermaking supplies and papers

Lee S. McDonald, Inc.
523 Medford Street
P.O. Box 264
Charlestown, Massachusetts 02129
(617) 242-2505
Papermaking supplies

Fred B. Mullet
2707 59th Street S.W. - Suite A
Seattle, Washington 98116
(206) 932-9482
Rubber stamps from nature prints

Nasco
901 Janesville Avenue
P.O. Box 901
Fort Atkinson, Wisconsin 53538-0901
(800) 558-9595
Art supplies and papers

Paper-Ya & Kakali Handmade Papers, Inc.
9-1666 Johnston Street
Granville Island
Vancouver, British Columbia
Canada V6H 3S2
(604) 684-2531
Papers

Pearl Paint Co. Inc.
308 Canal Street
New York, New York 10013-2572
(800) 451-PEARL
Art supplies and paper

Swallow Creek Papers
P.O. Box 152
Spring Mills, Pennsylvania 16875
(814) 422-8651
Decorative papers for papercrafts